THE PEOPLE
of
LOCHEL, CUSHNEY & KINBETACH (TOWIE)
1696

Taken from
List of Pollable Persons within
the Shire of Aberdeen 1696
Volume 1.

Presbytery of Alford

The Book or List off Poleable persons within the Shire off **Aberdein** & Burghs within the same

Containing the naimes off the haill persons poleable and Polemoney payable be them conforme to their respective capacities According to the Act off Parliament anent Polemoney dated the day of

Faithfullie extracted ffurth of the Principall Lists of poleable persons off each paroch within the Shyre as they were reported by the Comissioners and Clerks for the severall paroches appointed for that effect

By William Hay Collector appointed off the polemoney payable ffurth of the said shire

And revised and examined by ane Quorum of the Commissioners of Supplie off the saiden Shyre and attested by them

first day of Aprile 1696

This Book belongs to
Thomas Gordon of [illegible]

The title page from the '<u>List of Pollable Persons</u> '.

INTRODUCTION

During the late seventeenth century the Scottish economy cupboard was bare and the need for extra revenue was essential. One of the ways used was a tax on people - A POLL TAX - and several were collected during the 1690's. Supposedly a tax on every person over the age of sixteen not a beggar, although this has been disputed. Therefore for genealogical purposes an extant list of over 30,000 names from 1696 is of immense value. Even more so is the transcription and publication, in two volumes, of this unique document by the Gentlemen of the County in 1844. It is from this edition that our facsimile reprint comes, also included is a page from the original 1696 volume.

Anyone wishing to check the original will find it in Aberdeen University Archives (MS548). Our thanks must go to the staff of both the Archives and Special Collections departments of the University Library for their help. The photograph of the original is reproduced by kind permission of the Archives.

Although dated 1696 the date the lists were approved, in fact they were compiled in September 1695.

A history of the original volume is also interesting - it was in the library of Thomas Gordon of Buthlaw and his descendants till their fortunes failed and the estate was sold during the First World War. The book was then bought by Col. D.F. Davidson who donated it to Aberdeen University in the 1920's.

In the Special Collections department of the University (housed in the same building as the Archives) there exists an Index to the 'list' compiled in the 19th century by Dingwall Fordyce, however it is a very selective list consisting only of the more 'important' people. The index included here is comprehensive and also includes a place name index as well as an occupation breakdown.

Several points have to be made to make understanding this volume easier:

1) Any errors in the 1844 published version have been perpetuated in this edition.
2) The original page numbers of the 1844 edition have been used throughout.

LESLEY DIACK

LIST of POLEABLE PERSONS within the PAROCH of LOCHELL, given up be PATRICK FORBES *of Foullis, and* ALEXANDER GARIOCH *of Tilliechetlie, Commissioners appointed for the said Paroch, and be* JOHN DAVIDSONE *in Bridgend of Knockandach, Clerk and Collector appointed by them for the said Paroch.*

THE LAIRD of CRAIGIEVARR his valuatione within the paroch of Lochell is eight hundereth and fourtie one punds Scots..........£841 0 0

The hundereth part whereof is.. £8 9 2

Which is divided amongst the tennents as followes, viz. :—

	£	s.	d.
Alexander Garioch in Mains of Craigievarr, his proportion is....	£1	0	10
Alexander Ritchie, tennent in Westsyde, his proportion is	0	4	8
Alexander Thomsone, tennent ther, his proportione is.............	0	4	8
Alexander Coutts, tennent in Wester Lochell, his proportion is	0	9	4
John Smith, tennent in Brigs, his proportione is.....................	0	2	4
James Pantone, tennent in Hillock, his proportione is	0	4	8
Patrick Pantone, tennent ther, his proportione is.....................	0	4	8
William Michie, tennent in Upper Lochell, his proportione	0	9	4
William Mathiesone, tennent ther, his proportione is..............	0	4	8
John Mathiesone, tennent ther, his proportione is...................	0	4	8
Alexander Steven, tennent in Bandine, his proportione is.........	0	4	8
Andrew Johnstone, tennent at Milne of Craigievarr	0	4	8
George Galloway, at the Walk Milne of Craigievarr...............	0	4	8
William Touch in Knockandoch, his proportione is.................	0	9	4
Thomas Wright, tennent in Innenteir, his proportione............	0	9	4
Duncan Elsmie, tennent ther, his proportione is.....................	0	9	4
Patrick Gall, tennent ther, his proportione is.........................	0	4	8
John Yooll, tennent ther, his proportione is...........................	0	4	8
George Been, at Milne of Innenteir, his proportione	0	4	8
Andrew Been, tennent at Craigie Milne, his proportione	0	9	4
Alexander Roully, tennent in Wester Foullis, his proportione...	0	9	4
William Norie, tennent ther, his proportione is	0	4	8
William Forbes, tennent ther, his proportione is....................	0	4	8
William Wright, tennent in Bogend, his proportion is.............	0	4	8
Alexander Watt, tennent in Bogsyde, his proportione is	0	1	4
Andrew Massone, tennent in Hilend, his proportione...............	0	1	2
Alexander Luncart, tennent in Foullis, his proportione...........	0	2	4
Allaster Forrest, tennent ther, his proportione is....................	0	1	2
George Mettellen, tennent ther, his proportione......................	0	1	2

William Thomsone, tennent ther, his proportione is.................. 0 1 2
John Mitchell in Balvenie, his proportione is........................ 0 2 4
£8 10 2

(Item, Alexander Garioch, pollable for his valuatione in the paroch of Alfoord, wherein is included his proportione of his masters valuatione.)
Item, Barbara Forbes, his wife, her generall poll is.................................. £0 6 0
Item, William, Alexander, Patrick, Lodovick Gariochs, his sones, and Elizabeth Garioch, his daughter, ther generall poll is.............................. 1 10 0
Item, John Garioch, his servant, his fee is 22 merkes per annum, fortieth pairt whereof is 7s. 4d., and generall poll 6s., *inde* both is........................ 0 13 4
Item, John Reid, also his servant, his fee is 22 merkes per annum, fortieth part wherof is 7s. 4d., and generall poll 6s., *inde*.............................. 0 13 4
Item, Jeane Weir, his servant, her fee is £8 per annum, fortieth part wherof is 4s., and generall poll 6s., *inde*...................................... 0 10 0
Item, John Mackie, his fee is £8 per annum, fortieth part wherof is 4s., and generall poll 6s., *inde* both is.. 0 10 0
Item, Magdalen Ross, also his servant, her fee is £3 10s. per annum, fortieth part wherof 1s. 9d., and generall poll 6s., *inde*................................ 0 7 9
(All those above writtine servants are *in familia.*)
£4 10 5

The said Alexander Garioch his Subtennents are as followes:
Item, Thomas Cordoner in Craigievar (no stock, no trade), of generall poll is... £0 6 0
Item, Helen Ross, his wife, her generall poll is.................................. 0 6 0
James Mackie, subtennent in Craigievar (no trade), of generall poll.............. 0 6 0
Jannet Glennie, his wife, her generall poll is................................... 0 6 0
Item, William Mitchell, subtennent ther, and Elspet Wilkie, his wife, their generall poll.. 0 12 0
Item, Andrew Moir, gardener in Craigievarr, and Jannet Walker, his wife, their generall poll.. 0 18 0
Item, William Moir, his sone, and Margaret Moir, his daughter, their generall poll is... 0 12 0
£3 6 0

WESTSIDE.

Item, Alexander Ritchie, tennent ther, and Elspet Milne, his wife, their generall poll.. £0 12 0
Item, George Ogg, his servant, his fee is £16 per annum, fortieth pairt wherof is 8s., and generall poll 6s., *inde* both is................................ 0 14 0
Item, Anna Ritchie, also his servant, her fee is 10 merks per annum, fortieth pairt whereof is 3s. 4d., and generall poll 6s., *inde*.......................... 0 9 4
Item, James Cook, his servant, has no fee but meat and cloath, his generall poll... 0 6 0
Item, John Broune (no trade), subtennent to the said Alexander Ritchie, and Elspet More, his wife, their generall poll is................................ 0 12 0
Item, Margaret Hendrie, grasswoman, of generall poll 6s., *inde*................... 0 6 0

Item, ALEXANDER THOMSONE, tennent ther, and Margaret Mitchell, his wife, their generall poll	£0	12	0
Item, Margarat Cattanach, his servant, her fee is 10 merks per annum, fortieth pairt wherof is 3s. 4d., and generall poll 6s., *inde*	0	9	4
Item, Patrick Shirras, grasman ther, and Beatrix Foullar, his wife, their generall poll is	0	12	0
Item, John Thomsone, his hird, his fee is £3 per annum, fortieth part wherof is 1s. 6d., and generall poll 6s., *inde* both is	0	7	6
Item, James Garrioch ther, and Janet Michie, his wife, their generall poll is...	0	12	0
	£5	12	2

WESTER LOCHELL.

Item, Alexander Coutts, tennent ther, and Margaret Spens, his wife, their generall poll	£0	12	0
Item, John Coutts, his sone, of generall poll is	0	6	0
Patrick Patersone, his servant, his fee is £17 per annum, fortieth pairt whereof is 8s. 6d., and generall poll 6s., *inde* both is	0	14	6
Item, George Couper, also his servant, of fee 22 merks per annum, fortieth part wherof is 7s. 4d., and generall poll 6s., *inde*	0	13	4
Item, Patrick Touch, ane subtennent (no trade), his generall poll is	0	6	0
Item, Jeane Forbes, his wife, of generall poll	0	6	0
Item, James Smith, his herd, his fee is £5 per annum, fortieth pairt wherof is 2s. 6d., and generall poll 6s., *inde*	0	8	6
Item, JOHN SMITH tennent and blacksmith in Bridges of Lochell, his poll	0	12	0
Item, Elspet Coutts, his wife, her generall poll is	0	6	0
	£4	4	4

HILLOCK OF LOCHELL.

Item, John Pantone, tennent ther, and his wife, ther generall poll is	£0	12	0
Item, William Pantone, his son, of generall poll	0	6	0
Item, Alexander Forbes, subtennent ther, and Elspet Shaw, his wife, of generall poll is	0	12	0
Item, James Cranich (no trade), and Jeane Adam, his spous, ther generall poll	0	12	0
Item, Alexander Grant, subtennent ther (no trade), and Bethia Mitchell, his wife, ther generall poll is	0	12	0
Item, William Forbes sone to the said Alexander Forbes, his generall poll	0	6	0
Item, Patrick Pantone, tennent ther, and Jeane Mackenzie, his wife, ther geneall poll	0	12	0
Item, Robert Mitchell, his herd, his fee is £6 per annum, fortieth part wherof is 3s., and generall poll 6s., *inde* both is	0	9	0
Item, Arthur Kelles, subtennent (no trade), and Janet Tailleor, his wife, ther generall poll is	0	12	0
Item, John Trinit, ther (no trade, no wife), his generall poll is	0	6	0
	£4	19	0

UPPER LOCHELL.

Item, William Milne, tennent ther, and Jeane Ross, his wife, ther generall poll is	£0	12	0

	£	s.	d.
Item, William Forbes, his servant, of fee 26 merks per annum, fortieth part wherof is 8s. 8d., and generall poll 6s., *inde* both is	0	14	8
Item, John Jafferay, also his servant, his fee is £12 per annum, fortieth part wherof is 6s., and generall poll 6s., *inde* both is	0	12	0
Item, Margaret Gibbon, his servant, of fee £8 per annum, fortieth part wherof is 4s., and generall poll 6s., *inde* both is	0	10	0
Item, Alexander Thomsone, his herd, his fee is 8 merks per annum, fortieth part wherof is 2s. 8d., and generall poll 6s., *inde*	0	8	8
Item, James Thomsone, subtennent, and Elspet Brine, his wife, ther generall poll is	0	12	0
Isbell Edie, generall poll is	0	6	0
Item, George Mathiesone, his generall poll is	0	6	0
Item, Arthur Garioch, his subtennent ther, and Jeane Forbes, his wife, ther generall poll is	0	12	0
Item, James Mackie, his herd, his fee is £6 per annum, fortieth part wherof is 3s., and generall poll 6s., *inde* both is	0	9	0
WILLIAM MATHEWSON, tennent, and his wife	0	12	0
Item, JOHN MATHIESONE, tennent ther, and Margaret Galloway, his wife, ther generall poll	0	12	0
	£4	7	8

BANDINE.

	£	s.	d.
Item, Alexander Stevin, tennent ther, and Isobell Cruickshank, his wife, ther generall poll is	£0	12	0
Item, Charles Beine, his servant, his fee is £14 per annum, fortieth part wherof is 7s., and generall poll 6s., *inde*	0	13	0
Item, Robert Allan, his herd of fee 8 merks per annum, fortieth pairt whereof is 2s. 8d., and generall poll 6s., *inde* both is	0	8	8
	£1	13	8

CRAIGIEVARR.

	£	s.	d.
Item, Andrew Johnstone, millart ther, having no wife, his generall poll	£0	12	0
Item, Thomas Hendersone, his subtennent (no trade), and Janet Michie, his wife	0	12	0
Item, George Galloway at Walkmilne of Craigievarr, walker and tennent ther, of generall poll	0	12	0
Item, Agnes Couper, his mother, and Elizabeth Galloway, his sister, ther poll is	0	12	0
Item, John Johnstone, his servant, his fee is 14 merks per annum, fortieth part whereof is 4s. 8d., and generall poll 6s., *inde* both is	0	10	8
Item, William Touch, his hird, his fee is £6 per annum, fortieth part whereof is 3s., and generall poll 6s., *inde*	0	9	0
	£3	7	8

KNOCKANDACH.

	£	s.	d.
Item, William Touch, tennent ther, and Isobell Rae, his wife, their generall poll is	£0	12	0
Item, George Glennie, his hird, of fee £6 per annum, fortieth part whereof is 3s., and generall poll 6s., *inde*	0	9	0

Item, James Gordone, also his hird, his fee is £6 per annum, fortieth part whereof is 3s., and generall poll 6s., *inde* both is	£0	9	0
Item, Margaret Erskine, of fee £8 per annum, fortieth part whereof is 4s., and generall poll 6s., *inde* both is	0	10	0
Item, James Tough, subtennent and weaver, and Janet Meassone, his spouse, their poll is	0	18	0
Item, George Bruce, subtennent and weaver ther, and his wife, their generall poll	0	18	0
	£3	16	0

INNENTEIR.

Item, Thomas Tough, tennent ther, and Isobell Murray, his wife, their generall poll is	£0	12	0
Itam, William Tough, his sone, and Isobell Tough, his daughter, their generall poll is	0	12	0
Item, Alexander Clerk, his servant, his fee is 8 merks per annum, fortieth part whereof is 2s. 8d., and generall poll 6s., *inde*	0	8	8
Item, Isobell Low, grasswoman ther, her generall poll is	0	6	0
Item, Agnes Tough ther, her generall poll is	0	6	0
Item, PATRICK YOOLL, tennent ther, and Janet Stevene, his wife	0	12	0
Item, John Yooll and William Yooll, his sons, their generall poll is	0	12	0
Item, John Wilsone, grassman ther, and Elspet Tough, his wife	0	12	0
Item, DUNCAN ELSMIE, tennent in Innenteir, and Catharine Dune, his wife, their generall poll is	0	12	0
Item, Margaret Dasone, grasswoman ther, her generall poll is	0	6	0
Item, GEORGE BEINE, tennent at Milne of Innenteir, and milner to the said Milne, with Margaret Jamesone, his wife	0	18	0
Item, William Jaffray, his servant, of fee £12 per annum, fortieth part whereof is 6s., and generall poll 6s., *inde* both is	0	12	0
Item, Agnes Roy, also his servant, of fee 10 merks per annum, fortieth part whereof is 3s. 4d., and generall poll 6s., *inde*	0	9	4
	£6	18	0

CRAIGMILNE.

Item, Andrew Beine, tennent ther, and Agnes Clerk, his wife, their generall poll	£0	12	0
Item, William Jaffray, his servant, his fee is 26 merks per annum, fortieth part whereof is 8s. 8d., and generall poll 6s., *inde*	0	14	8
Item, William Mitchell, his grassman (no trade), and Margaret Ritchie, his wife, their generall poll is	0	12	0
	£1	18	8

WESTER FOULLIS.

Item, Alexander Ritchie, in Wester Foullis, and Isobell Tailleor, his wife, ther generall poll is	£0	12	0
Item, Isobell Ritchie, his daughter, her generall poll is	0	6	0
Item, William Fraser, his herd, of fee £6 per annum, fortieth part wherof is 3s., and generall poll	0	9	0

Item, Elspet Tailleor, grasswoman ther, of generall poll	£0	6	0
Item, Janet Hendersone, grasswoman ther, of generall poll	0	6	0
Item, WILLIAM NORIE, tennent and wright, his generall poll	0	12	0
Item, Janet Norie, his daughter, of generall poll	0	6	0
Item, Marjorie Kynzoach, of generall poll	0	6	0
Item, WILLIAM FORBES, tennent ther, and Elspet Broune, his wife, of generall poll is	0	12	0
John Crookshank, and Marjorie Mackie, his wife	0	12	0
	£4	7	0

BOGEND.

Item, Touch, tennent ther, and Jeane Ross, his wife, their generall poll	£0	12	0
Item, Agnes Ross, his servent, her fee is 10 merks per annum, fortieth part whereof is 3s 4d., and generall poll 6s., *inde*	0	9	4
Item, William Milne, his herd, of fee £5 per annum, fortieth part whereof is 3s., and generall poll 6s., *inde*	0	9	0
Item, William Cruickshank, subtennent and weaver ther, with Isobell Wallas, his wife, their poll is 18s., *inde*	0	18	0
Item, John Wright, subtennent ther (no trade), and Agnes Wright, his spous, their generall poll is	0	12	0
Item, Robert Fergus, cordoner ther, and Margaret M'Redie his wife, their generall poll is	0	18	0
	£3	18	4

BOGSYDE.

Item, Alexander Watt, tennent ther, and Elspet Allan, his wife, their poll	£0	12	0
Item, Margaret Reid, his good-daughter, of generall poll	0	6	0
Item, Andrew Meassone, tennent and tailleor in Hilhead, and Beatrix Luncart, his wife, their poll is	0	18	0
Item, Alexander Luncart, tennent in Foullis, and Issobell Mearnes, his wife, their generall poll is	0	12	0
Item, Allaster Forrest, tennent ther, and Elspet Watson, his wife, ther generall poll.	0	12	0
Item, George Maitland, tennent and weaver ther, his poll	0	12	0
Item, William Thomsone, tennent ther, and Janet Rae, his wife, their poll	0	12	0
Item, John Mitchell, tennent in Balvenie, and Janet Mitchell, his wife, their generall poll is	0	12	0
	£4	16	0

Item, Mr. ALEXANDER SETTONE, minister at Lochell, his poll is	£3	6	0
Item, John Tailleor, his servant, of fee £16 per annum, fortieth part whereof is 8s., and generall poll 6s., *inde* both is	0	14	0
Item, Margaret Cordoner, his servant, of fee £8 per annum, fortieth part whereof is 4s., and generall poll 6s., *inde*	0	10	0
Item, Margaret Macull, his servant, her fee is £8 per annum, fortieth pairt whereof is 4s., and generall poll 6s., *inde*	0	10	0
	£5	0	0

The valuatione of the LAIRD of FOULLIS land, within the paroch of Lochell, is three hundereth and seventie punds Scots........ £370 0 0

The hundereth part whereof is £3 14s........ £3 14 0

Which is divided amongst the tennents as follows, viz.:—

John Jaffray in the Maines of Foullis (no trade, no stock), his proportione of his masters valued rent is........	£1	8	6			
James Allardes, tennent in Upper Foullis, his proportione is....	0	14	0			
Patrick Robertsone, tennent ther, his propertione........	0	7	0			
James Laing, tennent ther, his proportione is........	0	7	0			
John Tough, tennent at Milne of Foullis, his proportione........	0	7	0			
John Rae, tennent ther, his proportione is........	0	7	0			
John Havour, tennent in Scutrie, his proportione........	0	4	0			
				3	14	6

(The Laird of Foullis is not pollable in this paroch, he being ane residenter in the paroch of Tough for the tyme.)

MAINES OF FOULLIS.

Item, John Jaffray, tennent ther, and Jeane Hunter, his wife, their poll........	£0	12	0
Item, Patrick Thomsone, his servant, of fee £20 per annum, fortieth pairt whereof is 10s., generall poll 6s., *inde*........	0	16	0
Item, George Clerk, also his servant, his fee is £18 per annum, fortieth pairt whereof is 9s., and generall poll 6s., *inde*........	0	15	0
Item, William Lawsone, his herd, his fee is £6 per annum, fortieth part whereof is 3s., and generall poll 6s., *inde*........	0	9	0
Patrick William, also his herd, his fee is £6 per annum, fortieth part whereof is 3s., and generall poll 6s., *inde*........	0	9	0
Item, Robert Clerk, his third herd, his fee is £6 per annum, fortieth part whereof is 3s., and generall poll 6s., *inde*........	0	9	0
Item, Elspet Bruce, his woman servant, her fee is £9 per annum, fortieth part whereof is 4s. 6d., and generall poll 6s........	0	10	6
Item, Allaster Essone, subtennent ther, and shoemaker, payes of poll........	0	12	0
Item, Christian Rora, his wife, her generall poll is........	0	6	0
Jannet Lasson, servitrix to said Jaffrey, £9 of fee, is, with generall poll........	0	10	6
Item, Elspet Hay, subtennent ther, her generall poll is........	0	6	0
Item, James Cook, subtennent ther, and Agnes Fergus, his wife, generall poll	0	12	0
Item, Agnes Buchan, grasswoman ther, her generall poll........	0	6	0
Item, Alexander Clerk, subtennent ther, and Margaret Ross, his wife, their generall poll........	0	12	0
	£7	5	0

UPPER FOULLIS.

James Allardes, tennent ther, and Jeane Elsmie, his wife, their poll........	£0	12	0
Item, Christian Home, his servant, her fee is £6 per annum, fortieth part wher-of is 3s., and generall poll 6s., *inde*........	0	9	0

Item, Robert Reid, subtennent ther, and Agnes Thomson, his wife, their poll... £0 12 0

Item, William Farquhar, subtennent ther, and Agnes Reid, his spouse, their generall poll 0 12 0

Item, Patrick Robertsone, tennent in Upper Foullis, and Margaret Thomsone, his wife, their generall poll 0 12 0

Item, James Laing, tennent ther, and Janet Riach, his wife, their generall poll is 0 12 0

£3 9 0

MILNE OF FOULLIS.

Item, John Tough, tennent ther, and Christian Anderson, his wife, their generall poll is £0 12 0

Item, William Coutts, his servant, his fee is £8 per annum, fortieth pairt wherof is 4s., and generall poll 6s., *inde* 0 10 0

Item, Agnes Tough, his servant, her fee 10 merks per annum, fortieth pairt whereof is 3s. 4d., and generall poll 6s........ 0 9 4

Item, John Rae, tennent ther, and Catharine Bonar, his wife, their poll is...... 0 12 0

Item, Duncan Tailleor, his servant, his fee is £8 per annum, fortieth part whereof is 4s., and generall poll 6s. 0 10 0

Item, William Ferries, subtennent and tailleor ther, and Beatrix Jamesone, his wife, their poll 0 18 0

Item, Andrew Measson, subtennent (no trade), and Catharine Thomsone, his wife, their generall poll 0 12 0

Item, John Havour, tennent in Scuterey (no trade nor stock), and Isobell Hendrie, his wife, their generall poll 0 12 0

£4 15 4

Patrick Forbes of Foullis, factor for the Laird of Lenturk, gave up the Laird and his Tennents as followes :—

Imprimis, The Laird of Lenturk himselfe, being above fiftie punds of valued rent, and under two hundreth punds, notwithstanding he is not residenter in the paroch, yet being classed in the highest capacity, he is pollable for his above written valuatione in the soume of four punds, and generall poll 6s. £4 6 0

The said Lenturk his valuatione being £120 .... £120 0 0

The hundreth part whereof is £1 4s. 6d. £1 4 6

Which is divided among the tennents as followes, viz. :—

Andrew Farquhar in Mains of Lenturk, his proportione........ £0 10 0

James Coupland in Clemill, his proportione is........ 0 8 0

James Skene in Drumdarge, his proportione is........ 0 6 0

£1 4 0

MAINES OF LENTURK.

Imprimis, Andrew Farquhar, tennent ther, of generall poll £0 6 0

Item, Alexander Lawsone, gardener ther, and Mary Stool, his wife £0 18 0
Item, John Forbes, tennent, and smith to his trade, with his wife, Grissel Leightoune, their poll 0 18 0
Item, George Miller, subtennent ther (of no trade), and Margaret Cruckshank, his wife, their generall poll 0 12 0

£2 14 0

CLEMILL.

Item, James Coupland, tennent ther, and Isobell Watt, his wife, their poll...... £0 12 0
Robert Coupland, his sone, his generall poll 0 6 0
Item, William Andersone, subtennent ther (no trade), his generall poll........... 0 6 0

£1 4 0

DRUMDARGE.

James Skene, tennent ther (no trade), and Elspet Wilsone, his wife, their generall poll £0 12 0

JOHN GORDONE of Edintor, not being residenter within this paroch, is not pollable here himselfe; but his valuatione in the said paroch being two hundreth and fourtie punds.............. £240 0 0

The hundreth pairt wherof is £2 8s. £2 8 0

Which is divided among the tennents as followes, viz. :—

John Baxter at Bridgend of Knockandach, his proportion.........	£0	4	0
Andrew Lawsone, tennent at Milne of Lenturk, his proportion...	0	10	0
William Mitchell, tennent in Litle Lenturk, his proportione......	0	8	0
Andrew Gregorie, tennent ther, his proportion..............	0	8	0
James Elsmie, tennent in Mugarthaugh, his proportion............	0	2	0
Thomas Urquhart, tennent in the Fermtoun of Lenturk............	0	8	0
James Urquhart, his sone, tennent ther, his proportion	0	8	0

2 8 0

BRIDGEND OF KNOCKANDACH.

Imprimis, John Baxter, tennent ther, and Isobell Buck, his wife, their generall poll.............. £0 12 0
Item, William Allan, his servant, his fee is 22 merks per annum, fortieth part whereof is 7s. 4d., and generall poll 6s., *inde* both is 0 13 4
Item, Elizabeth Weir, his woman servant, her fee is 14 merks per annnm, fortieth part whereof is 4s. 8d., and generall poll 6s., *inde*.............. 0 10 8

£1 16 0

MILNE OF LENTURK.

Item, Andrew Lawsone, tennent ther, of generall poll.............. £0 6 0
Item, John Laing, his servant, his fee is 22 merks per annum, fortieth part wherof is 7s. 4d., and the generall poll. 6s., *inde*.............. 0 13 4
Item, Robert Jamesone, his hird, of fee 10 merks per annum, fortieth part wherof is 3s. 4d., and generall poll 6s., *inde*.............. 0 9 4
Item, Alexander Broune, subtennent (no trade), and Janet Dune, his wife, their generall poll.............. 0 12 0

	£	s.	d.
Item, John Lawsone, subtennent ther, and weaver, with his wife, Christian Gordone, their poll is	£0	18	0
Item, Margaret Irvine, relict of the deceist Lewis Gordon of Belnastryne, being lyable for the third part of her said deceist husbands poll as ane gentlemen, which would have bein £3, she is lyable, as said is, in £1, and generall poll 6s	1	6	0
Item, Mary Irvine, her sister, generall poll is	0	6	0
Item, John Pullor, subtennent (of no trade), his generall poll is	0	6	0
	£4	16	8

LITLE LENTURK.

	£	s.	d.
Item, William Mitchell, tennent ther, and Elspet Stevine, his spouse, their generall poll is	£0	12	0
Item, Andrew Gregorie, tennent ther, and Ephey Smith, his spouse, their generall poll is	0	12	0
Item, Charles Gregorie, his servant, his fee is 8 merks per annum, fortieth pairt wherof is 4s. 8d., and generall poll 6s., *inde*	0	8	8
Item, James Elsmie, tennent in Mougerth Haugh, and Jannet Tough, his spouse, their generall poll	0	12	0
	£2	4	8

FERMTOUN OF LENTURK.

	£	s.	d.
Item, Thomas Urquhart, tennent ther, and Christian Reid, his wife, their generall poll is	£0	12	0
Item, Patrick Urquhart, his sone, his generall poll	0	6	0
Item, William Jamesone, his hird, his fee is 8 merks per annum, fortieth pairt wherof is 2s. 8d., and generall poll 6s., *inde*	0	8	8
Item, Agnes Stivine, his servant, her fee is £6 per annum, fortieth part wherof is 3s., and generall poll 6s	0	9	0
Item, James Urquhart, tennent ther, of generall poll	0	6	0
Item, John Gordone, his hird, his fee is 8 merks per annum, fortieth part wherof is 2s. 8d., and generall poll 6s., *inde*	0	8	8
Item, Robert Jamesone, subtennent ther (no trade), and Elspet Clerk, his wife, their generall poll	0	12	0
Item, Thomas Lawsone, shoemaker ther, and Isobell Sutter, his spouse, their poll	0	18	0
Item, Elspet Tailleor, ane grasswoman ther, of generall poll	0	6	0
Item, Alexander Urquhart, subtennent ther (no trade), and Elspet Reid, his spouse, their generall poll	0	12	0
Item, Alexander Pillor, subtennent and weaver ther, and Christian Robertsone, his wife, their poll is both	0	18	0
	£5	16	4

	£	s.	d.
Summa of LEOCHELL paroch is	£119	9	3

PARISH OF LOCHELL

NAME (both sexes)	PAGE
ADAM Jeane	428
ALLAN Elspet	431
Robert	429
William	434
ALLARDES James	432(2)
Jeane	432
ANDERSON Christian	433
ANDERSONE William	434
BAXTER Isobell	434
John	434(2)
BEEN Andrew	426
George	426
BEINE Agnes	430
Andrew	430
Charles	429
George	430
Margaret	430
BNAR Catharine	433
BRINE Elspet	429
BROUNE Alexander	434
Elspet	427,431
Janet	434
John	427
BRUCE Elspet	432
George	430
BUCHAN Agnes	432
BUCK Isobell	434
CATTANACH Margarat	428
CLERK Agnes	430
Alexander	430,432
Elspet	435
George	432
Margaret	432
Robert	432
COOK Agnes	432
James	427,432
CORDONER Helen	427
Margaret	431
Thomas	427
COUPER Agnes	429
George	428
COUPLAND Isobell	434
James	433,434
Robert	434
COUTTS Alexander	426,428
Elspet	428
John	428
Margaret	428
William	433
CRAIGIEVARR Laird of	426
CRANICH James	428
Jeane	428
CROOKSHANK John	431
Marjorie	431
CRUCKSHANK Margaret	434
CRUICKSHANK Isobell	429,431
William	431
DASONE Margaret	430
DAVIDSONE John	426
DUNE Catharine	430
Janet	434
EDIE Isbell	429
ELSMIE Catharine	430
Duncan	426,430
James	434,435
Jannet	435
Jeane	432
ERSKINE Margaret	430
ESSONE Allaster	432
Christian	432
FARQUHAR Agnes	433
Andrew	433(2)
William	433
FERGUS Agnes	432
Margaret	431
Robert	431
FERRIES Beatrix	433
William	433
FORBES Alexander	428(2)
Barbara	427
Elspet	428,431
Grissel	434
Jeane	428,429
John	434
Patrick	426,433
William	426,428,429,431
FORREST Allaster	426,431
Elspet	431
FOULLAR Beatrix	428
FOULLIS Laird of	432(2)
FRASER William	430
GALL Patrick	426
GALLOWAY Elizabeth	429
George	426,429
Margaret	429
GARIOCH Alexander	426(2),427(3)
Arthur	429
Barbara	427
Elizabeth	427
Jeane	429
John	427
Lodovick	427

PARISH OF LOCHELL

NAME (both sexes)	PAGE
GARIOCH Patrick	427
William	427
GARRIOCH James	428
Janet	428
GIBBON Margaret	429
GLENNIE George	429
Jannet	427
GORDON Lewis	435
Margaret	435
GORDONE Christian	435
James	430
John	434,435
GRANT Alexander	428
Bethia	428
GREGORIE Andrew	434,435
Charles	435
Ephey	435
HAVOUR Isobell	433
John	432,433
HAY Elspet	432
HENDERSONE Janet	429,431
Thomas	429
HENDRIE Isobell	433
Margaret	427
HOME Christian	432
HUNTER Jeane	432
IRVINE Margaret	435
Mary	435
JAFFERAY John	429
JAFFRAY Jeane	432
John	432(2)
William	430(2)
JAFFREY Male	432
JAMESONE Beatrix	433
Elspet	435
Margaret	430
Robert	434,435
William	435
JOHNSTONE Andrew	426,429
John	429
KELLES Arthur	428
Janet	428
KYNZOACH Marjorie	431
LAING James	432,433
Janet	433
John	434
LASSON Jannet	432

NAME (both sexes)	PAGE
LAWSONE Alexander	434
Andrew	434(2)
Christian	435
Isobell	435
John	435
Mary	434
Thomas	435
William	432
LEIGHTOUNE Grissel	434
LENTURK Laird of	433(3)
LOW Isobell	430
LUNCART Alexander	426,431
Beatrix	431
Issobell	431
MACKENZIE Jeane	428
MACKIE James	427,429
Jannet	427
John	427
Marjorie	431
MACULL Margaret	431
MAITLAND George	431
MASSONE Andrew	426
MATHEWSON William	429
MATHIESONE George	429
John	426,429
Margaret	429
William	426
MCREDIE Margaret	431
MEARNES Issobell	431
MEASSON Andrew	433
Catharine	433
MEASSONE Andrew	431
Beatrix	431
Janet	430
METTELLEN George	426
MICHIE Janet	428,429
William	426
MILLER George	434
Margaret	434
MILNE Elspet	427
Jeane	428
William	428,431
MITCHELL Bethia	428
Elspet	427,435
Janet	431
John	427,431
Margaret	428,430
Robert	428
William	427,430,434,435
MOIR Andrew	427
Jannet	427

PARISH OF LOCHELL

NAME (both sexes)	PAGE
MOIR Margaret	427
William	427
MORE Elspet	427
MURRAY Isobell	430
NORIE Janet	431
William	426,431
OGG George	427
PANTONE James	426
Jeane	428
John	428
Patrick	426,428
William	428
PATERSONE Patrick	428
PILLOR Alexander	435
Christian	435
PULLOR John	435
RAE Catharine	433
Isobell	429
Janet	431
John	432,433
REID Agnes	433(2)
Christian	435
Elspet	435
John	427
Margaret	431
Robert	433
RIACH Janet	433
RITCHIE Alexander	426,427(2),430
Anna	427
Elspet	427
Isobell	430(2)
Margaret	430
ROBERTSONE Christian	435
Margaret	433
Patrick	432,433
RORA Christian	432
ROSS Agnes	431
Helen	427
Jeane	428,431
Magdalen	427
Margaret	432
ROULLY Alexander	426
ROY Agnes	430
SETTONE Alexander	431
SHAW Elspet	428
SHIRRAS Beatrix	428
Patrick	428

NAME (both sexes)	PAGE
SKENE Elspet	434
James	433,434
SMITH Elspet	428
Ephey	435
James	428
John	426,428
SPENS Margaret	428
STEVEN Alexander	426
STEVENE Janet	430
STEVIN Alexander	429
Isobell	429
STEVINE Elspet	435
STIVINE Agnes	435
STOOL Mary	434
SUTTER Isobell	435
TAILLEOR Duncan	433
Elspet	431,435
Isobell	430
Janet	428
John	431
THOMSON Agnes	433
THOMSONE Alexander	426,428,429
Catharine	433
Elspet	429
James	429
Janet	431
John	428
Margaret	428,433
Patrick	432
William	427,431
TOUCH Isobell	429
Jeane	428,431
Male	431
Patrick	428
William	426,429(2)
TOUGH Agnes	430,433
Christian	433
Elspet	430
Isobell	430(2)
James	430
Janet	430
Jannet	435
John	432,433
Thomas	430
William	430
TRINIT John	428
URQUHART Alexander	435
Christian	435
Elspet	435
James	434,435

PARISH OF LOCHELL

NAME (both sexes)	PAGE
URQUHART Patrick	435
Thomas	434,435
WALKER Jannet	427
WALLAS Isobell	431
WATSON Elspet	431
WATT Alexander	426,431
Elspet	431
Isobell	434
WEIR Elizabeth	434
Jeane	427
WILKIE Elspet	427
WILLIAM Patrick	432
WILSONE Elspet	430,434
John	430
WRIGHT Agnes	431
John	431
Thomas	426
William	426
YOOLL Janet	430
John	426,430
Patrick	430
William	430

PARISH OF LOCHELL

OCCUPATIONS

Blacksmith	1
Clerk & Collector	1
Commissioner	2
Cordoner	1
Factor	1
Gardener	2
Grassman	3
Grasswoman	7
Herd or Hird	17
Laird	3
Millart or Milner	2
Minister	1
Servant Female	15
Servant Male	22
Servitrix	1
Shoemaker	2
Smith	1
Tailleor	2
Walker	1
Weaver	6

PARISH OF LOCHELL

PLACE NAME		PAGE
ALFOORD		427
BALVENIE		427,431
BANDINE		426,429
BELNASTRYNE		435
BOGEND		426,431
BOGSYDE		426,431
BRIGS		426
CLEMILL		433,434
CRAIGIE MILNE		426
CRAIGIEVAR		427(2)
CRAIGIEVARR		426,427,429
	Mains of	426
	Milne of	426
	Walkmilne of	426,429
CRAIGMILNE		430
DRUMDARGE		433,434
EDINTOR		434
FOULLIS		426(2),431,432(2),433
	Maines of	432(2)
	Milne of	432,433
	Upper	432(2),433
	Wester	426,430(2)
HILEND		426
HILHEAD		431
HILLOCK		426
INNENTEIR		426,430(2)
	Milne of	426,430
KNOCKANDACH		429
	Bridgend of	426,434(2)
KNOCKANDOCH		426
LENTURK		433(3)
	Fermtoun of	434,435
	Litle	434,435
	Mains of	433(2)
	Milne of	434(2)
LOCHELL		426(2),431,432,435
	Bridges of	428
	Hillock of	428
	Upper	426,428
	Wester	426,428
MOUGERTH HAUGH		435
MUGARTHAUGH		434
SCUTEREY		433
SCUTRIE		432
TILLIECHETLIE		426
TOUGH		432
WESTSIDE		427
WESTSYDE		426

POPULATION

MALES	160
FEMALES	116
TOTAL	276

LIST of the POLLABLE PERSONS within the PAROCH of CUSHNEY, given up be ALEXANDER LUMSDELL *of Cushney, and* JOHN GORDONE *of Hallhead, Commissioners appointed for the said Paroch, and be* MR. GEORGE KERR, *Clerk and Collector appointed be them for the said Paroch.*

IMPRIMIS, the VALUATIONE of the whole paroch is........................£923 5 0

The LAIRD of CUSHNEYES valuatione in the said paroch is.....................£586 11 8

The hundreth pairt whereof is.. £5 17 4
(*Nota.*—This is not devyded amongst the tennents in the poll list given up, but is to be payed be the heretor in a soume.)

Cushneyes own Familie.

	£	s.	d.
The Laird of Cushney and his lady, is of poll	£12	12	0
Item, David and Lodwick Lumsdens, his sones, their poll is	3	0	0
Item, Elizabeth Lumsden, his daughter, her generall poll is	0	6	0
Item, Thomas Lumsden, his servant, his fee is £16 per annum, fortieth pairt whereof is 8s., and the generall poll 6s., *inde* both is..................	0	14	0
Item, William Gordone, his servant, getts no fee except cloaths, *inde*............	0	6	0
Item, John Ædie, also his servant, no fee except cloaths, *inde*......................	0	6	0
Item, Charles William, servant, gets no fee but cloaths, *inde*........................	0	6	0
Item, Lucriss Forbes, his servant, her fee is £6 per annum, fortieth pairt with generall poll, is..	0	9	0
Item, Barbray Murgan, also his servant, of fee £6 per annum, fortieth pairt, with generall poll, is..	0	9	0
Item, Rachell Watt, servant, her fee is £4, fortieth pairt, with generall poll, is	0	8	0
Item, Alexander Weddell, gardner, and Elspet Turner, his spouse, poll is.......	0	18	0
	£19	14	0

The Tennents Names belonging to the Laird of Cushney in the said paroch :— John Smith in Cairncoully; Arthur Hosie in Drumifatty; John Hosie in Burnend; Alexander Leas, William Forbes, Peter Ross, James Morgan, John Couts, George William, John Fledger, in Minmorres; John Forbes, Alexander William, in Pitprone; William Rae, John Tow, Eupheme Fyfe, in Elshillocks; Duncane Burnet, John Wilsone, Robert Riach, John Robertsone, William Dassone, David Ferras, in Bennakelley; James Lumsden, William Ross, John Riach, Alexander Riach, in Balchimmy; George Laing, Alexander Tough, John Patersone, Jannet Broune, in Milnetoune; Robert Boge, William Dassone, Thomas Mortimer, William Boge, James Morgane, in

Knockriach; William Morgane in Brideswall; William Mitchell, Alexander Smith, in Kirktoune; William Tauese in Wark; Alexander Bonner in Ley.

CAIRNCOULLY.

Imprimis, John Smith, tennent ther, and his wife, ther generall poll is	£0	12	0
Item, Patrick Smith, his sone, his generall poll is	0	6	0
Item, George Smith, his servant, his fee 20 merks per annum, the fortieth pairt wherof is 6s. 8d., and the generall poll of 6s., *inde* both is	0	12	8
Item, William Kelles, servant, fee is 8 merks per annum, fortieth pairt wherof and generall poll	0	8	8
Item, Jannet Smith, servant, her fee is 8 merks per annum, fortieth pairt with generall poll, is	0	8	8
Item, Jean Crearer, servant, her fee is 8 merks per annum, fortieth pairt with generall poll	0	8	8
	£2	16	8

MINMORES.

Item, Alexander Leas, tennent ther, and Jannet Burnet, his spouse, ther poll is	£0	12	0
Item, William Forbes, tennent ther, and Isobel Rae, his wife, ther poll is	0	12	0
Item, Peter Ross, weaver, and Margrat Bog, his spouse, ther poll is	0	18	0
Item, James Morgan, tennent ther, and Margrat Toshach, his wife, ther poll is	0	12	0
Item, George William, tennent ther, and Margrat Rae, his wife, ther poll	0	12	0
Item, John Couts, tennent ther, his generall poll is	0	6	0
Item, John Fledger, tennent ther, and Anna Murgane, his wife, ther generall poll	0	12	0
	£4	4	0

PITPRON.

Item, John Forbes, tennent ther, and Jannet Burnet, his wife, ther generall poll,	£0	12	0
Item, Alexander William, tennent ther, and Christane Sanders, his wife, ther generall poll	0	12	0
	£1	4	0

DRUMFATTY.

Item, Arthur Hossie, tennent ther, his generall poll is	£0	6	0
Item, James Hossie, his brother-german, his generall poll is	0	6	0
	£0	12	0

BURNEND.

Item, John Hossie, tennent ther, and Christane Andersone, his wife	£0	12	0

ELSHILLOCKS.

Item, William Rae, tennent ther, and Issobell Tough, his wife, ther poll is	£0	12	0
Item, James Rae, his sone, his generall poll is	0	6	0
Item, John Tough, weaver ther, and Marjorie Wishart, his wife, their poll is	0	18	0
Item, Euphane Fyfe, tennent ther, hir generall poll is	0	6	0
	£2	2	0

BELNAKELLY.

Item, Duncan Burnet, tennent ther, and his wife, their generall poll is	£0	12	0
Item, John Wilsone, tennent ther, and Issobell Ferres, his wife, their poll	0	12	0
Item, Robert Riach, tennent ther, and Elspet Patersone, his wife, their generall poll	0	12	0
Item, John Robertsone, tennent ther, and Isobel Dasson, his wife, poll	0	12	0
Item, William Dasson, tennent ther, and Margrat Smith, his wife	0	12	0
Item, David Ferres, tennent ther, and Elspet Mitchell, his wife, poll	0	12	0
Item, John Glennie, weaver ther, and Margrat Clerk, his wife, poll	0	18	0
Item, John Robertsone, elder ther, his generall poll is	0	6	0
	£4	16	0

BALCHIMMY.

Item, James Lumsden, tennent ther, and Issobell Fraser, his wife, their poll	£0	12	0
Item, Elspet Taues, his servant, hir fee is £4 per annum, fortieth pairt, with generall poll	0	8	0
Item, William Ross, farmer ther, and Jannet Patersone, his wife, their poll is	0	12	0
Item, John Riach, tennent ther, and Margaret Couts, his wife, their generall poll is	0	12	0
Item, Alexander Riach, tennent ther, his generall poll is	0	6	0
Item, Robert Ross ther, his generall poll is	0	6	0
	£2	16	0

MILTOUNE.

Item, George Lainge, millart ther, and his wife, their generall poll is	£0	18	0
Item, Alexander Lainge, his son, his generall poll is	0	6	0
Item, Jean Lainge, his daughter, hir generall poll is	0	6	0
Item, James Traill, younger, his servant, his fee £4 per annum, fortieth pairt, with generall poll	0	8	0
Item, Alexander Tough, weaver, and Anna Riach, his wife, their generall poll is	0	18	0
Item, John Patersone, shoemaker, and his wife, their poll is	0	18	0
Item, Jannet Brown, tennent ther, hir generall poll is	0	6	0
	£4	0	0

KNOCKRIACH.

Item, Robert Bog, tennent ther, and his wife, their generall poll is	£0	12	0
Item, William Dasson, tennent ther, and Issobell Robertsone, his wife	0	12	0
Item, Thomas Mortimer, tennent ther, and Christane Wilsone, his wife, their poll	0	12	0
Item, William Bog, tennent ther, and Jean Bandone, his wife, their generall poll is	0	12	0
Item, James Morgan, tennent ther, and his wife, their poll is	0	12	0
Item, George Wilsone, taylor ther, and his wife, their generall poll is	0	18	0
Item, William Rait, grassman ther, and his wife, their poll is	0	12	0
Item, John Mitchell ther, his generall poll is	0	6	0
	£4	16	0

BRIDSWALL.

Item, William Morgan, tennent ther, his generall poll is	£0	6	0
Item, Christane M'Robie, his servant, hir fee 8 marks per annum, fortieth pairt and generall poll	0	8	0
	£0	14	8

KIRKTOUNE.

Item, William Mitchell, tennent ther, and Jean Nivie, his wife, their poll,	£0	12	0
Item, Alexander Smith, blacksmith ther, and Jannet Ross, his wife, ther poll is	0	18	0
Item, Margaret Smith, her daughter, her generall poll is	0	6	0
	£1	16	0

WARKE.

Item, William Tause, tennent ther, and Agnes Reid, his wife, ther poll is	£0	12	0
Item, Peter Tause, his sone, his generall poll is	0	6	0
Item, Elspet Tause, his daughter, her generall poll is	0	6	0
Item, George Ingrame, his servant, his fee is £10 per annum, fortieth pairt with generall poll	0	11	1
Item, Francis Forbes, servant, gets no fee, but cloaths, his generall poll is	0	6	0
	£2	1	0

LEY.

Item, Alexander Bonner, tennent ther, and his wife, their generall poll is	£0	12	0
Item, Alexander Dassone, his servant, his fee is £10 per annum, fortieth pairt whereof and generall poll	0	11	0
Item, Margrat William, his servant, her fee is 9 merks, fortieth pairt with generall poll	0	7	4
	£1	10	4

List of the pollable persons within the Laird of Craigievarrs lands in the paroch of Cushney.

The Laird of CRAIGIEVARS valuatione within the said paroch is eighty punds, Scots	£80	0	0
The hundreth pairt whereof is 16s.	£0	16	0

(*Nota.*—This is not divided amongst the tennents in the Poll List given up, but is to be payed be the heritor in a soume.)

CULMELLY.

Imprimis, John Tough, tennent ther, and his wife, their generall poll	£0	12	0
Item, William Robertsone, his servant, his fee is £16 per annum, the fortieth pairt wherof is 8s., and generall poll 6s., *inde* both is	0	14	0
Item, James Ramsay, servant, his fee £2 per annum, fortieth pairt, with generall poll	0	7	0
Item, Jannet Fyfe, his servant, her fee is 10 merks per annum, fortieth pairt and generall poll	0	9	4

The parish of LEOCHEL CUSHNIE c 1696

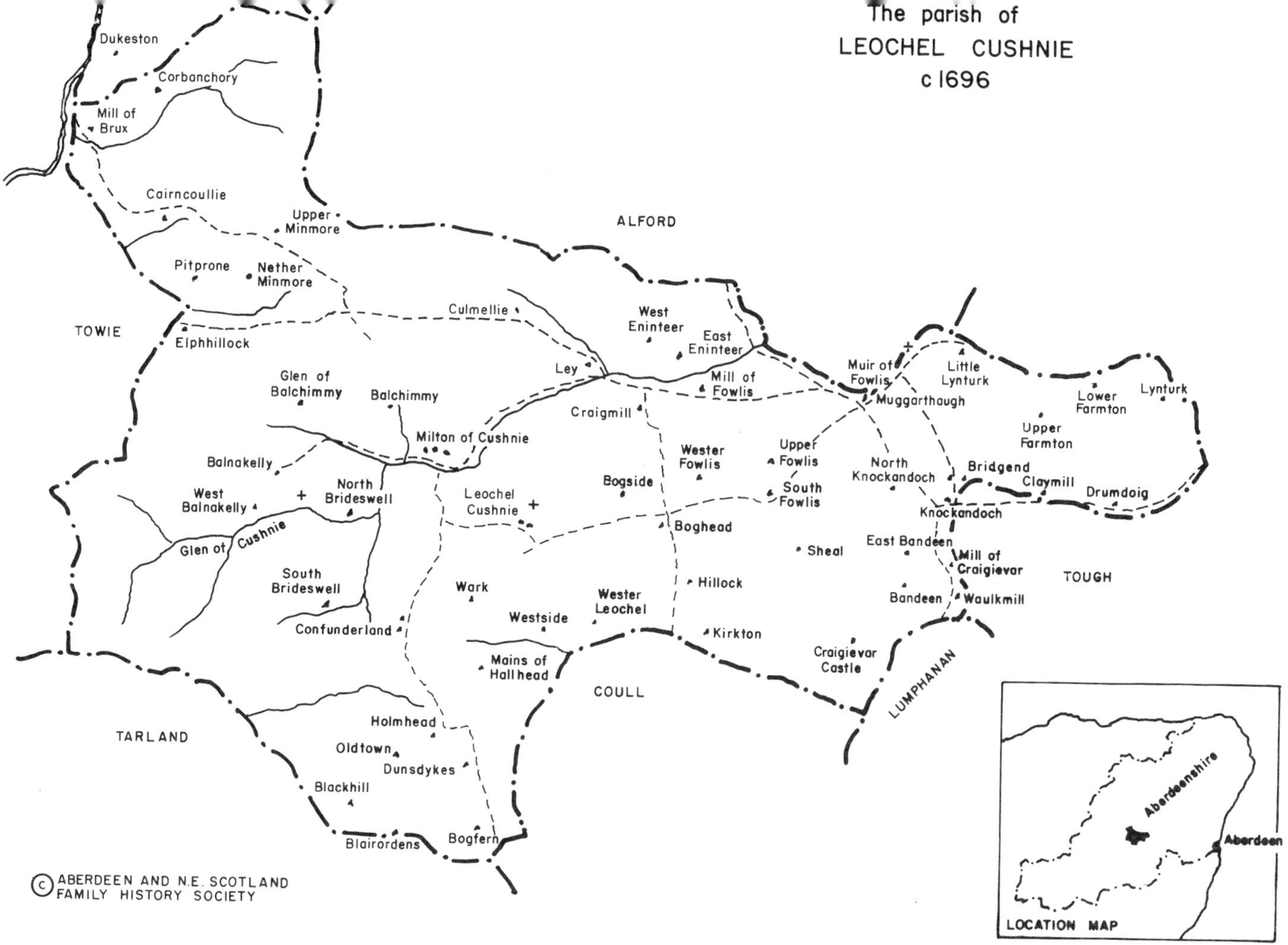

The parish of TOWIE

c 1696

The name Towie is derived from the Gaelic *'Tuaidh'* meaning "north lying land"
The ancient name of Towie parish was Kinbethock a corruption of Kilbartha or Bartha's Cell

On 15 May 1891 a detached part of Strathdon parish along with a small detached part of Tarland and Migvie parish was added to the parish of Towie

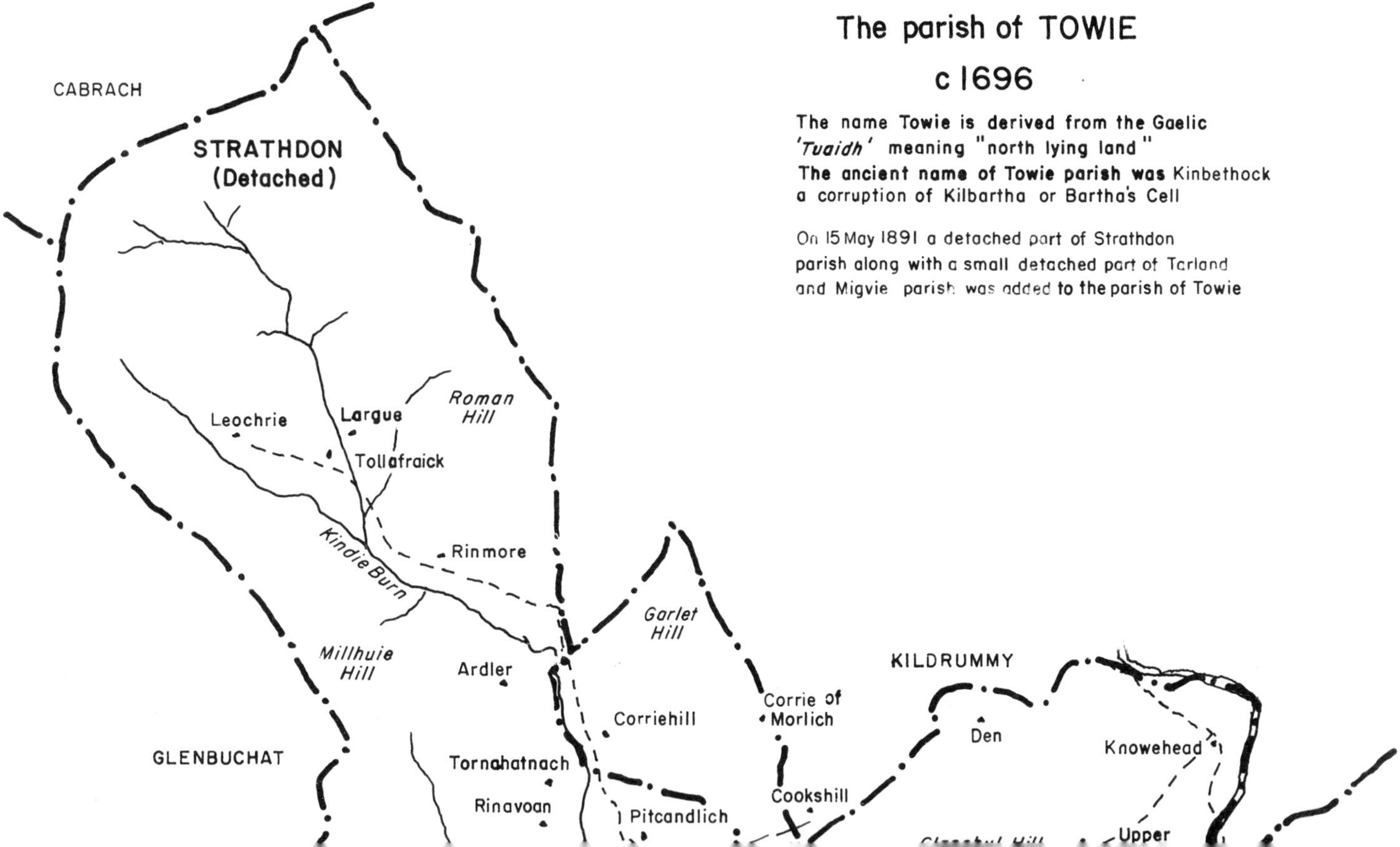

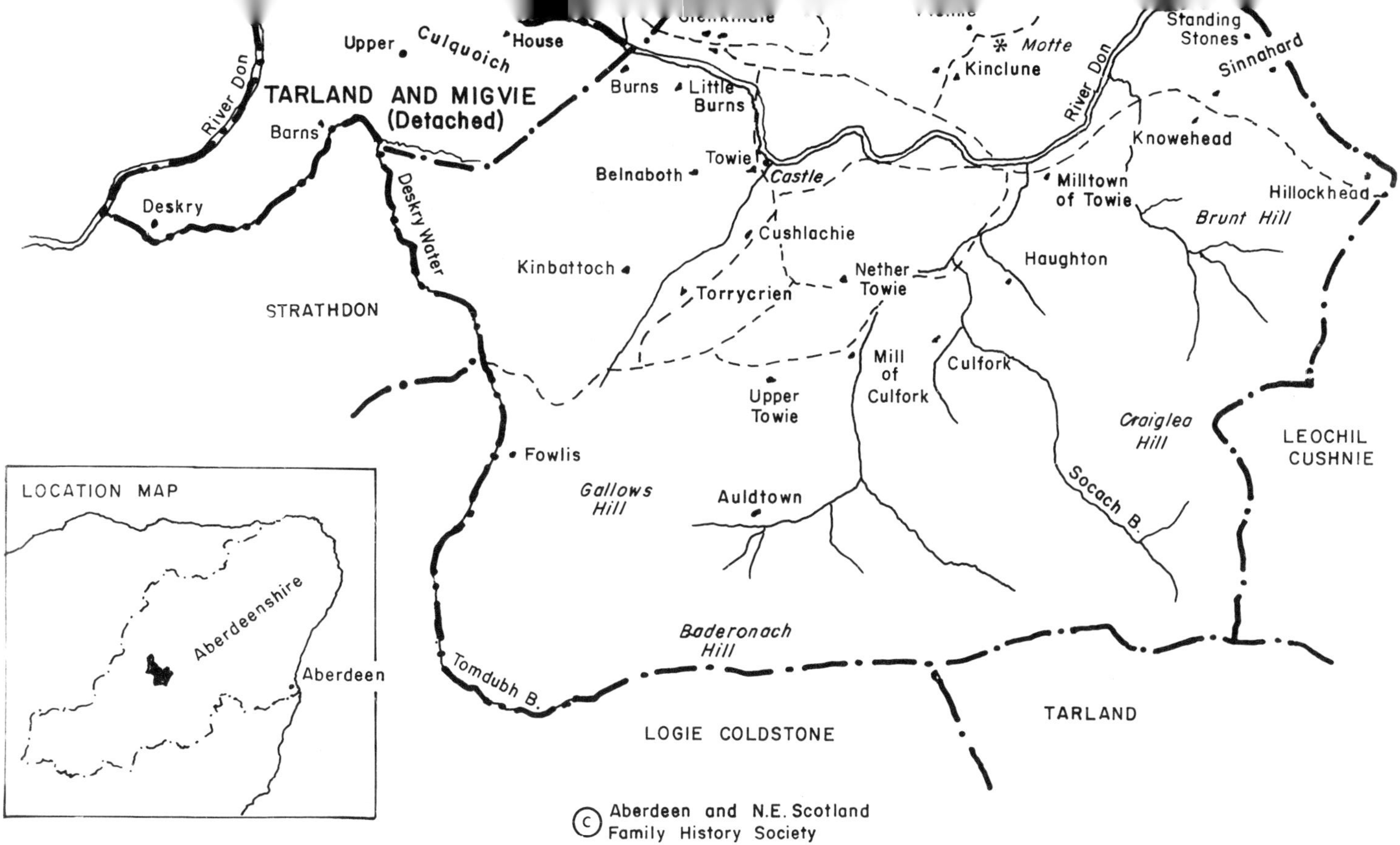

Upper Culquoich
House
TARLAND AND MIGVIE
(Detached)
River Don
Barns
Deskry
Deskry Water
STRATHDON
Burns
Little Burns
Towie
Castle
Belnaboth
Kinbattoch
Cushlachie
Torrycrien
Nether Towie
Kinclune
Motte
Standing Stones
Sinnahard
Knowehead
Milltown of Towie
Hillockhead
Brunt Hill
Haughton
Mill of Culfork
Culfork
Upper Towie
Craiglea Hill
LEOCHIL CUSHNIE
Socach B.
Fowlis
Gallows Hill
Auldtown
Baderonach Hill
Tomdubh B.
LOGIE COLDSTONE
TARLAND
LOCATION MAP
Aberdeenshire
Aberdeen
© Aberdeen and N.E. Scotland Family History Society

Item, William Touch, tennent ther, and his wife, their generall poll is	£0	12	0
Item, Charles Watt, his servant, his fee is £4 per annum, fortieth pairt, with generall poll	0	8	0
Item, Alexander Willocks, servant, his fee is £4 per annum, fortieth pairt, with generall poll	0	8	0
	£3	10	4

List of all the pollable persons in the Laird of Hallhead his lands, in the paroch of Cushney.

The Laird of HALLHEAD his valuatione within the paroch is ane hundreth and sixtie six pound thirtein shilling fourpennies Scots money	£100	13	4
The hundreth pairt whereof is £1 13s. 4d.	£1	13	4

(*Nota.*—This is not devyded amongst the tennents in the Poll List given up, but it is to be payed be the heritor in a soume.)

Hallheads owen Familie.

Imprimis, the Laird of Hallhead payes of poll for himselfe and ladie	£9	12	0
Item, Patrick, Robert, and William Gordons, his sones, their poll is	0	18	0
Item, Patrick Gordone, his brother, payes of poll	3	6	0
Item, Charles Gordone, his brother, payes of poll	3	6	0
Item, Margrat Gordone, his mother, her generall poll is	3	6	0
Item, Margrat and Marie Gordons, his sisters, their generall poll is	0	12	0
Imprimis, Peter Ego, his servant, his fee £21 per annum, fortieth pairt whereof is 10s., and generall poll 6s., *inde* both is	0	16	0
Item, Alexander Gordone, his servant, his fee is £13 per annum, fortieth pairt whereof is 6s. 6d., and generall poll 6s., *inde*	0	12	6
Item, Patrick M'William, servant, his fee is £8 per annum, fortieth pairt whereof is 4s., and generall poll 6s., *inde*	0	10	0
Item, Peter Norrie, servant, his fee 8 merks per annum, fortieth pairt whereof, with generall poll	0	8	8
Item, John M'Grigore, servant, his fee £4 16s. per annum, fortieth pairt, with generall poll	0	8	4
Item, Elspet Wattie, servant, hir fee is £10 per annnm, fortieth pairt, with generall poll, is	0	11	4
Item, Margrat Binnie, servant, hir fee is £11 per annum, fortieth pairt, with generall poll	0	11	6
Item, Jean Carney, servant, hir fee is £4 per annum, fortieth pairt, with generall poll, is	0	8	0
	£25	6	0

His Tennents names as followes :—James Taillyour in Tilligray; Peter Ogilvie in Rickie, shoemaker; John Fraser in Munroe, shoemaker; John Rawer ther; John Milne in Brayhead; Alexander Suttor in

Dwnsdykes ; George Murgan in Bogfarne ; Robert Ross, ther ; Peter Tawese in Blair Ordens ; Robert Smith in Blackhills ; Jannet Midletoune in Oldtoune ; George Suttor in Hollinhead ; William Tawese in Curfunderland ; Thomas Tawese ther ; Duncane Tause ther.

TILLIGRAY.

Imprimis, James Taillyour, tennent ther, and his wife, their generall poll is......	£0	12	0
Item, Patrick Ogilvie, shoemaker in Rickie, and his wife, poll is..................	0	18	0
	£1	10	0

MUNROE.

Item, John Fraser, shoemaker ther, and his wife, their poll is......................	£0	18	0
Item, John Rawer, cottar, and his wife, their generall poll is.......................	0	12	0
Item, John Milne, tennent in Brayhead, and his wife, their generall poll is......	0	12	0
Item, Alexander Suttor, tennent in Dunsdykes, his generall poll is................	0	6	0
Item, John Smith, his servant, his fee is £4, fortieth pairt with generall poll is	0	8	0
	£2	16	0

BOGFAIRNE.

Item, George Murgan, tennent ther, and his wife, their generall poll is..........	£0	12	0
Item, James Beg, weaver ther, and his wife, their poll is............................	0	18	0
Item, Elspet Ord ther, her generall poll is..	0	6	0
Item, Robert Ross, tennent ther, and his wife, their generall poll is...............	0	12	0
Item, Allan Smith, cottar ther, and his wife, their generall poll is..................	0	12	0
	£3	0	0

BLAIRORDENSE.

Item, Patrick Tauese, tennent ther, and his wife, their generall poll is...........	£0	12	0
Item, Lewes Litljohn, his servant, his fee is £12, fortieth pairt with generall poll..	0	12	0
Item, Anna Dassone, servant, her fee is £6 per annum, fortieth pairt with generall poll	0	9	0
Item, Robert Smith, blacksmith, in Blackhills, and his wife, their poll is.........	0	18	0
Item, Robert Smith, his sone, his generall poll is..	0	6	0
Item, William M'William, servant, his fee is £8 per annum, fortieth pairt with generall poll..	0	10	0
	£3	7	0

OLDTOUN.

Item, Jannet Midletoune, tennent ther, her generall poll is..........................	£0	6	0
Item, Alexander Skeen, her sone, his generall poll is..................................	0	6	0
Item, George Suttor, tennent in Holinhead, and his wife, their generall poll is...	0	12	0
	£1	4	0

CURFUNDERLAND.

Item, Duncan Tauese, tennent ther, and his wife, their poll is......................	£0	12	0
Item, James Litlejohn, his servant, his fee per annum is 16 merks, the fortieth pairt whereof is 5s. 4d., and generall poll 6s., *inde*..............................	0	11	4
Item, Margrat Shirres, her fee is £4 per annum, fortieth pairt with generall poll	0	8	0

Item, Thomas Tause, tennent ther, and his wife, their generall poll is	£0	12	0
Item, William Tause, tennent ther, and his wife, their generall poll is	0	12	0
Item, Alexander M'William, tennent ther, and his wife, their generall poll is	0	12	0
	£3	7	4

List of all the polable persons within the Laird of Brux his lands in the parochin of Cushney.

The Laird of BRUX valuatione within the said paroch is nyntie pounds, Scots money	£90	0	0
The hundreth pairt whereof is	£0	18	4

(*Nota.*—This is not devyded amongst the tennents in the poll list given up, but is to payed be the heritor in a soume.)

CURBANCHRIE.

Item, John William, tennent ther, and Elspet Ross, his wife, their generall poll,	£0	12	0
Item, Robert Watt, his servant (gets no fee), his generall poll is	0	6	0
Item, George Hosie, tennent ther, and his wife, ther generall poll is	0	12	0
Alexander Reid and Barbra Majer, his servants, gets no fee	0	12	0
Alexander Hosie, tennent ther, and his wife, their generall poll	0	12	0
Item, Thomas Gordone, weaver ther, and his wife, their generall poll is	0	18	0
Item, George Umphry, weaver ther, and his wife, their generall poll is	0	18	0
Item, Elspet Andersone ther, her generall poll is	0	6	0
Item, Jannet Couts ther, her generall poll is	0	6	0
Item, Elspet Reid ther, her generall poll is	0	6	0
	£5	8	0

STANDING STONES.

Item, Alexander M'Lachlan, tennent ther, and his wife, their generall poll is	£0	12	0

DUKESTONE.

Item, Walter Kinerd, gentleman ther, his poll is	£3	6	0
Item, John Henderson, his servant, his fee is £10 per annum, fortieth pairt whereof is 5s., and generall poll 6s., *inde* both is	0	11	0
Item, John Thomsone, servant (gets no fee), his generall poll is	0	6	0
Item, John Taues ther, his generall poll is	0	6	0
Item, Donnald Dumbar ther, his generall poll is	0	6	0
Item, Agnes Dumbar ther, her generall poll is	0	6	0
Item, Issobell Dune ther, her generall poll is	0	6	0
Item, Christane Tailyour ther, her generall poll is	0	6	0
Item, Jean Couper ther, her generall poll	0	6	0
Item, Francis Mair ther, and his wife, their generall poll is	0	12	0
Item, James Fyfe ther, and his wife, their generall poll is	0	12	0
Item, John Gordone ther, his generall poll is	0	6	0
	£7	9	0

List of the pollable persons within the Minister of Cushney's familie, as followes :—

	£	s.	d.
Imprimis, he gives up himselfe to be eightie nyn pounds, Scots money, of valued rent, in the paroch of Oyne, and is lyable in four pound Scots of poll ...	£4	6	0
Item, Jean Gordon, his wife, her generall poll is	0	6	0
Item, John, Charles, and William Couplands, his sones, their poll is	0	18	0
Item, Agnes, Margrat, Elizabeth, and Mary Coplands, his daughters, their poll is	1	4	0
Item, Patrick Michie, his servant, his fee is £16 per annum, fortieth pairt, with generall poll, is	0	14	0
Item, William Ædie, servant (gets no fee), his generall poll is	0	6	0
Item, Margrat Murgan, servant, her fee is £6 per annum, fortieth pairt, with generall poll, is	0	9	0
Item, Issobell Broune, her fee is £4 per annum, fortieth pairt, with generall poll is	0	8	0
	£8	11	0
Summa of CUSHNEY paroch is	£129	0	8

POPULATION

MALES	125
FEMALES	99
TOTAL	224

PARISH OF CUSHNY

NAME (both sexes)	PAGE
AEDIE John	436
William	443
ANDERSONE Christane	437
Elspet	442
BANDONE Jean	438
BEG James	441
BINNIE Margrat	440
BOG Jean	438
Margrat	437
Robert	438
William	438
BOGE Robert	436
William	436
BONNER Alexander	437,439
BROUNE Issobell	443
Jannet	436
BROWN Jannet	438
BRUX Laird of	442(2)
BURNET Duncan	438
Duncane	436
Janet	437(2)
CARNEY Jean	440
CLERK Margrat	438
COPLAND Agnes	443
Elizabeth	443
Margrat	443
Mary	443
COUPER Jean	442
COUPLAND Charles	443
Jean	443
John	443
( ) Minister	443
William	443
COUTS Jannet	442
John	436,437
Margaret	438
CRAIGIEVAR Laird of	439
CRAIGIEVARR Laird of	439
CREARER Jean	437
CUSHNEY Lady of	436
Laird of	436(3)
Minister of	443
DASSON Isobel	438
Issobell	438
Margrat	438
William	438(2)
DASSONE Alexander	439
Anna	441

NAME (both sexes)	PAGE
DASSONE William	436(2)
DUMBAR Agnes	442
Donald	442
DUNE Issobell	442
EGO Peter	440
FERRAS David	436
FERRES David	438
Elspet	438
Issobell	438
FLEDGER Anna	437
John	436,437
FORBES Francis	439
Isobel	437
Jannet	437
John	436,437
Lucriss	436
William	436,437
FRASER Issobell	438
John	440,441
FYFE Euphane	437
Eupheme	436
James	442
Jannet	439
GLENNIE John	438
Margrat	438
GORDON Jean	443
Margrat	440
Marie	440
Patrick	440
Robert	440
William	440
GORDONE Alexander	440
Charles	440
John	436,442
Margrat	440
Patrick	440
Thomas	442
William	436
HALLHEAD Lady of	440
Laird of	440(3)
HENDERSON John	442
HOSIE Alexander	442
Arthur	436
George	442
John	436
HOSSIE Arthur	437
Christane	437

PARISH OF CUSHNY

NAME (both sexes)	PAGE
HOSSIE James	437
John	437
INGRAME George	439
KELLES William	437
KERR George	436
KINERD Walter	442
LAING George	436
LAINGE Alexander	438
George	438
Jean	438
LEAS Alexander	436,437
Jannet	437
LITLEJOHN James	441
LITLJOHN Lewes	441
LUMSDELL Alexander	436
LUMSDEN David	436
Elizabeth	436
Issobell	438
James	436,438
Lodwick	436
Thomas	436
MAIR Francis	442
MAJER Barbra	442
MCGRIGORE John	440
MCLACHIAN Alexander	442
MCROBIE Christane	439
MCWILLIAM Alexander	442
Patrick	440
William	441
MICHIE Patrick	443
MIDLETOUNE Jannet	441(2)
MILNE John	440,441
MITCHELL Elspet	438
Jean	439
John	438
William	437,439
MORGAN James	436,437,438
Margrat	437
William	439
MORGANE James	436
William	437
MORTIMER Christane	438
Thomas	436,438
MURGAN Barbray	436
George	441(2)
Margrat	443
MURGANE Anna	437

NAME (both sexes)	PAGE
NIVIE Jean	439
NORRIE Peter	440
OGILVIE Patrick	441
Peter	440
ORD Elspet	441
PATERSONE Elspet	438
Jannet	438
John	436,438
RAE Isobel	437
Issobell	437
James	43
Margrat	437
William	436,43
RAIT William	438
RAMSAY James	439
RAWER John	440,441
REID Agnes	439
Alexander	442
Barbra	442
Elspet	442
RIACH Alexander	436,43
Anna	43
Elspet	43
John	436,43
Margaret	43
Robert	436,43
ROBERTSONE Isobel	43
Isobell	43
John	436,438(2
William	439
ROSS Elspet	44
Jannet	438,439
Margrat	43
Peter	436,43
Robert	438,441(2
William	436,43
SANDERS Christane	43
SHIRRES Margrat	44
SKEEN Alexander	44
SMITH Alexander	437,43
Allan	44
George	43
Jannet	437,43
John	436,437,44
Margaret	43
Margrat	43
Patrick	43

PARISH OF CUSHNY

NAME (both sexes)	PAGE
SMITH Robert	441(3)
SUTTOR Alexander	440,441
George	441(2)
TAILLYOUR James	440,441
TAILYOUR Christane	442
TAUES Elspet	438
John	442
TAUESE Duncan	441
Patrick	441
William	437
TAUSE Agnes	439
Duncane	441
Elspet	439
Peter	439
Thomas	442
William	439,442
TAWESE Peter	441
Thomas	441
William	441
THOMSONE John	442
TOSHACH Margrat	437
TOUCH William	440
TOUGH Alexander	436,438
Anna	438
Issobell	437
John	437,439
TOUGH Marjorie	437
TOW John	436
TRAILL James	438
TURNER Elspet	436
UMPHRAY George	442
WATT Charles	440
Rachell	436
Robert	442
WATTIE Elspet	440
WEDDELL Alexander	436
Elspet	436
WILLIAM Alexander	436,437
Charles	436
Christane	437
Elspet	442
George	436,437
John	442
Margrat	437,439
WILLOCKS Alexander	440
WILSONE Christane	438
George	438
Issobell	438
John	436,438
WISHART Marjorie	437

PARISH OF CUSHNY

OCCUPATIONS

Blacksmith	2
Farmer	1
Gardener	1
Grassman	1
Millar	1
Servants	41
Shoemaker	3
Weaver	6

PARISH OF CUSHNY

PLACE NAME	PAGE
BALCHIMMY	436,438
BELNAKELLY	438
BENNAKELLY	436
BLACKHILLS	461(2)
BLAIRORDENS	441
BLAIRORDENSE	441
BOGFAIRNE	441
BOGFARNE	441
BRAYHEAD	440,441
BRIDESWALL	437
BRIDSWALL	439
BRUX	442
BURNEND	436,437
CAIRNCOULLY	436,437
CULMENY	439
CURBANCHRIE	442
CURFUNDERLAND	441(2)
CUSHNEY	436
DRUMFATTY	437
DRUMIFATTY	436
DUKESTONE	442
DUNSDYKES	441
DWNDYKES	441
ELSHILLOCKS	436,437
HALLHEAD	436,440
HOLINHEAD	441
HOLLINHEAD	441
KIRKTOUNE	437,439
KNOCKRIACH	437,438
LEY	437,439
MILNETOUNE	436
MILTOUNE	438
MINMORES	437
MINMORRES	436
MUNROE	440,441
OLDTOUN	441
OLDTOUNE	441
OYNE	443
PITRON	437
PITRONE	436
RICKIE	440,441
STANDINGSTONES	442
TILLIGRAY	440,441
WARK	437
WARKE	439

POPULATION

MALES	168
FEMALES	126
TOTAL	294

LIST of POLLABLE PERSONES within the PAROCH of KINBETACH, given up be Mr. JOHN INNES *of Calquhich, and* CHARLES INNES *of Belnaboth, Commissioners appointed for the said Paroch, and be* JOHN FORBES *in Towie, Clerk and Collector appointed be them for the said Paroch.*

THE VALUATION of the parioch of KINBETACH is........................£1475 7 2

The valuatione of the LADY DUAGER of MARR her interest in the said parioch is £364 7s. 2d. £364 7 2

The hundreth part whereof is £3 12 0

(*Nota.*—This is undivyded amongst the tennents in the poll list given up, but it is to be peyed be the Lady Marr, or her Chamberlanes, in a soume.)

(The Lady Marr does not receed within the said parioch, and therefor is not pollable for her familie ther.)

UPPER DRUMALACHIE.

Imprimis, John Bandon, tennent and widower ther, for himself of poll	£0	6	0
Item, Charles Fyfe, his servant, fee is £6 13s. 4d. per annum, fortieth pairt whereof is 3s. 4d., and generall poll 6s., *inde* both is	0	9	4
Item, Robert Gibbon, tennent ther, and Jannet Bulky, his spouse, generall poll,	0	12	0
Item, George Duncan, his servant, his fee is £6 13s. 4d. per annum, fortieth pairt whereof is 3s. 4d., and generall poll 6s., *inde* both is	0	9	4
Item, Christian Candach, widow woman, her generall poll is	0	6	0
Item, William Touch, widower ther, his generall poll is	0	6	0
Item, Alexander Tomb, his sone, his poll is	0	6	0
Item, George Wilsone, his servant, his fee is £4 per annum, fortieth pairt whereof is 2s., and generall poll 6s., *inde* both is	0	8	0
	£3	2	8

LEY.

Item, Patrick Bandan, tennent ther, and Margaret Gibbon, his spouse	£0	12	0
Item, Margaret Walker, his servant, her fee is £6 per annum, fortieth pairt whereof is 3s., and generall poll 6s., both is	0	9	0
Item, John Henderson, tennent ther, and Barbara Glenny, his spouse	0	12	0
Item, William Reid, tennent ther, and Christian M'Robie, his spouse	0	12	0
Item, Robert Beittie, his servant, his fee is £6 per annum, fortieth pairt wherof is 3s., and generall poll 6s., both is	0	9	0
Item, Alexander Walker, tennent ther, his generall poll is	0	6	0
Item, Andrew Walker, his son, his generall poll is	0	6	0
Item, Robert Reid, tennent ther, and Jean Riach, his spouse, their generall poll is	0	12	0
	£3	18	0

NETHER DRUMALACHIE.

Item, William Forbes, tennent ther, and Margaret Crimon, his spouse	£0	12	0
Item, Alexander Mortimer, his servant, his fee is £13 13s. 4d. per annum, fortieth pairt wherof is 6s. 10d., and generall poll 6s., both is	0	12	10
Item, William Mair, his servant, his fee £13 13s. per annum, fortieth pairt whereof is 6s. 10d., and generall poll 6s., both is	0	12	10
Item, Margaret Lamon, servant to the within designed William Forbes, her fee is £6 per annum, fortieth pairt wherof is 3s., and generall poll 6s., both is	0	9	0
Item, Elspet Smith, his servant, her fee £6 per annum, fortieth pairt whereof is 3s., and generall poll 6s., both is	0	9	0
	£2	15	8

KNOWHEAD.

Item, William Gibbon, tennent ther, and Margaret Ritchy, his spouse, generall poll	£0	12	0
Item, John Mitchell, tennent in Fuchlie, and Christian Mitchell, his sister	0	12	0
Item, James Mortimer ther, and Margaret Bredy, his spouse	0	12	0
Item, James Dason, tennent ther, and Elspet Bandon, his spouse	0	12	0
Item, Duncan Brody, tennent ther, and Elspet Munzie, his spouse	0	12	0
Item, John Brody, his sone	0	6	0

Item, William Watt, tennent in Den, and Jannet Dason, his wife, their poll	£0	12	0
Item, Patrick Strachan, tennent in Cookhill, and Margaret Kells, his spouse......	0	12	0
Item, William Yool, tennent ther, and Isobell Raeburn, his spouse	0	12	0
Item, Patrick Reid, shoemaker in Blairs, and Marjorie Bonnar, his wife	0	18	0
Item, James Thomson, notar publict in Corrihill, his poll is......................	4	6	0
Item, Marjorie Gordon, his spouse..	0	6	0
Item, William Fyfe, his servant, his fee is £10 13s. 4d., per annum, fortieth part whereof is 5s. 4d., and generall poll 6s., both is......................	0	11	4
Item, William Clerk, weaver ther, his poll is.......................................	0	12	0
Item, George Clerk, weaver ther, and his brother-german, his poll is.............	0	12	0
	£12	7	4

NEW MORLICHIE.

Item, Thomas Strachen, tennent ther, and Anna Reid, his spouse..................	£0	12	0
Item, Thomas Glenny, tennent ther, and Margaret Couts, his spouse............	0	12	0
Item, Alexander Dason, weaver ther, and Elspet Leitch, his wife, their poll...	0	18	0
Item, Patrick Leith, tennent ther, and Issobell Reid, his spouse.....................	0	12	0
Item, Patrick Forbes, tennent ther, and Mary Couts, his wife, their generall poll	0	12	0
Item, Charles Strachan, tennent in Old Morlichie, his generall poll is............	0	6	0
Item, John Gordone, tennent ther, and Margaret Reid, his spouse, generall poll is	0	12	0
Item, Agnes Reid, widow ther, her generall poll.......................................	0	6	0
Item, John Watt, tennent ther, and Marjorie Walker, his wife......................	0	12	0
Item, William Clerk, tennent ther, and Isobell Cook, his spouse, their poll......	0	12	0
Item, Isobell Morgan, cottar woman ther..	0	6	0
Item, Alexander Innes, tennent in Newbigging, and Lucriss Gray, his wife......	0	12	0
Item, Thomas Beitty his servant, his fee £13 13s. 4d. per annum, fortieth part whereof is 6s. 10d., and generall poll 6s. both is..............................	0	12	10
Item, Robert Coutts his servant, his fee £13 13s. 4d. per annum, fortieth part whereof is 6s. 10d., and generall poll 6s., both is............................	0	12	10
Item, John Gow, his herd, his fee is £6 per annum, fortieth part whereof is 3s., and generall poll 6s., both is	0	9	0
Item, James Shirraff, subtennent ther, and Margaret Law, his wife...............	0	12	0
	£8	17	8

The Laird of Brux his valuatione within the said parioch is four hundreth and eighty six pound, Scots money..	£486	0	0
The hundreth pairt whereof is..	£4	17	0

(*Nota.*—This is not devyded amongst the tennents in the poll list given up, but is to be peyed be the heretor in a soume.)

(The Laird of Brux doth not receed within the said parioch, and is not pole-able heir.)

MILNE OF TOWIE.

Item, John Reid, tennent ther, generall poll is..	£0	6	0

Item, John Coupland, millar ther, and Margaret Forbes, his spouse	£0	18	0
Item, Alexander Anderson, tennent in Culfork, his generall poll is	0	6	0
Item, Margaret Ross, his wife, her generall poll is	0	6	0
Item, James Anderson, his servant, his fee is £8 per annum, fortieth pairt wherof is 4s., and generall poll 6s., both is	0	10	0
Item, James Reid, tennent ther, and Margaret Reid, his spouse, their poll	0	12	0
Item, Alexander Craigie, tennent ther, his generall poll is	0	6	0
	£3	4	0

MILNE OF CULFORK.

Item, Arthour Forbes, gentleman, tennent ther, and Elspet Forbes, his spouse, their generall poll is	£3	12	0
Item, William Forbes, his sone, his poll is	0	6	0
Item, William Forbes, his servant, his fee is £10 per annum, fortieth pairt wherof is 5s., and generall poll 6s., both is	0	11	0
Item, Walter M'Farland, his servant, his fee is £6 per annum, fortieth pairt wherof is 3s., and generall poll 6s., both is	0	9	0
Item, William Anderson, tennent in Stycrofts, and Elspet Reid, his spouse	0	12	0
Item, John Craigie, tennent in the Old Toune, and Jannet Walker, his spouse,	0	12	0
Item, Alexander Elmslie, tennent ther, and Isobell Forbess, his spouse	0	12	0
Item, William Law, tennent ther, and Margaret Glass, his wife	0	12	0
Item, Alexander Thomson, tennent in Uper Towie, and Beatrix Grassiach, his wife	0	12	0
Item, John Walker, tennent ther, and Elspet Anderson, his wife	0	12	0
Item, Adam Berry, tennent ther, and Margaret Hendry, his spouse	0	12	0
Item, William Reid, tennent ther, and Jannet Reid, his spouse	0	12	0
Item, James Sumer, cottar ther, and Isobell Craigie, his spouse	0	12	0
Item, Alexander Bredy, weaver ther, and Jannet Bredy, his wife	0	18	0
Item, John Don, weaver ther, and Isobell Coutts, his spouse, their generall poll	0	18	0
	£12	2	0

FOULES.

Item, Alaster Coutts, weaver ther, and Jannet Connen, his wife	£0	18	0
Item, Alaster M'Grigor, tennent ther, and Elspet Wright, his spouse	0	12	0
Item, John Ferrer, weaver ther, and Isobell Robertson, his wife	0	18	0
Item, Alaster Glassian, tennent in Torriecarn, and Marjorie Forbes, his wife	0	12	0
Item, Arthour Glassian, tennent ther, and Jannet Alexander, his wife	0	12	0
Item, William Duncan, tennent in Cushlaihie, and Elspet Ritchy, his wife	0	12	0
Item, Alexander Walker, tennent ther, and Anna Dunbar, his spouse	0	12	0
Item, Thomas Grant, notar publict in Closhcunie, his poll is	4	6	0
Item, Jean Craigie, his spouse, her poll is	0	6	0
Item, John Coutts, weaver ther, and Elspet Morgan, his spouse	0	18	0
	£10	0	0

NETHER TOWY.

Item, Arthour Thomson, tennent ther, his generall poll	£0	6	0
Item, George Duncan, his servant, his fee is £12 per annum, fortieth pairt wherof is 6s., and generall poll 6s., both is	0	12	0

Item, Jean Laing, his servant, her fee is £6 per annum, fortieth pairt wherof is 3s., and generall poll 6s., both is	£0	9	0
Item, Alexander Messer, tennent ther, and Jean Michy, his wife, their generall poll is	0	12	0
Item, Robert Anderson, his servant, his fee is £12 per annum, fortieth pairt whereof is 6s., and generall poll 6s., both is	0	12	0
Item, James Duncan, tennent ther, and Christian Stephan, his wife	0	12	0
Item, Alaster Duncan, his sone	0	6	0
Item, Robert Duncan, tennent ther, and Beatrix Grassiach, his wife	0	12	0
Item, Arthur Toshech, his servant, his fee is £12 per annum, fortieth part whereof is 6s., and generall poll 6s., *inde*	0	12	0
Item, George Jaffray, tennent ther, and Janet Cowie, his wife	0	12	0
Item, Adam Murison, tennent in Maines of Towie, his generall poll is	0	6	0
Item, Margaret Tailzior, his spouse	0	6	0
Item, Marjorie Murison, his daughter, her generall poll is	0	6	0
Item, Ewan Murison, tennent ther, and Jannet Grassiach, his spouse	0	12	0
Item, Alaster Raine, his servant, his fee is £10 per annum, fortieth part whereof is 5s., and generall poll 6s., *inde*	0	11	0
	£7	6	0

The Laird of Craigivars valuatione with the parioch of Kinbetach is two hundereth and sixtie pound Scots	£260	0	0
The hundreth pairt whereof is	£2	12	0

(*Nota.*—This is not divided among the tennents in the poll list given up, but is to be payed by the heretor in a soume.)

(The Laird of Craigivar does not receed in this parioch, and therefor is not poleable heir.)

HAUGHTOUNE.

Item, John Shaw, tennent ther, and Jean Forbes, his wife	£0	12	0
Item, George Munzie, his servant, his fee is £13 6s. 8d. per annum, fortieth part whereof is 6s. 8d., and generall poll, *inde*	0	12	8
Item, William Wright, his servant, his fee is £10 per annum, fortieth part whereof is 5s., and generall poll 6s.	0	11	0
Item, Isobell Couts, his servant woman, her fee is £6 per annum, fortieth part whereof is 3s., and generall poll 6s.	0	9	0
	£2	4	8

SINABOTH.

Item, Alexander Dinkison, tennent ther, and Agnes Alexander, his wife	£0	12	0
Item, John Dinkison, his son, and Jeane Dinkison, his daughter, their generall poll	0	12	0
Item, Arthur Forbes, tennent ther, and Isobell Thomson, his wife	0	12	0
Item, James Luncart, tennent ther, and Elspet Panton, his spouse	0	12	0
Item, Alexander Forbes, tennent ther, and Elspet Kerr, his spouse	0	12	0

Item, Jean Forbes, his daughter	£0	6	0
Item, William Nairn, servant, her fee is £13 6s. 8d., per annum, fortieth part whereof is 6s. 4d., and generall poll 6s., both is	0	12	4
Item, James William, tennent ther, and Agnes Smith, his spouse	0	12	0
Item, John and George Williams, his sones, their generall poll	0	12	0
Item, Jannet Adam, his servant, her fee is £6 per annum, fortieth part whereof is 3s., and generall poll 6s., both is	0	9	0
Item, Lachlan Milne, tennent in Sunahards, Anna Forbes, his wife	0	12	0
Item, Margaret Forbes, his mother, her generall poll is	0	6	0
Item, John Forbes, servant, his fee being £10 per annum, fortieth part whereof is 5s., and generall poll 6s., *inde*	0	11	9
Item, Patrick Smith, tennent ther, and Margaret Cook, his spouse	0	12	0
Item, Francis Ferrer, his servant, fee is £10 per annum, fortieth pairt whereof is 5s., and generall poll 6s., both is.	0	11	0
Item, Alexander Thomson, tennent ther, and Jannet Duwie, his wife	0	12	0
Item, Arthur Thomson, tennent ther, and Isobell Knight, his wife	0	12	0
Item, William Dun, his servant, his fee is £12 per annum, fortieth part whereof is 6s., and generall poll 6s., both is	0	12	0
Item, John Morgan, tennent ther, and Isobell Michell, his spouse	0	12	0
	£10	11	8

UPPER SUNAHARD.

Item, Alexander Coutts, tennent ther, and Isobell Baxter, his wife, generall poll	£0	12	0
Item, George William, tennent ther, and Margaret Coutts, his wife	0	12	0
Item, John and Alexander Williams, his sones, their generall poll is	0	12	0
Item, Jannet Toshech, his servant, her fee is £6 per annum, fortieth pairt wherof is 3s., and generall poll 6s., both is	0	9	0
Item, George Bredy, tennent ther, and Christian Coutts, his spouse	0	12	0
Item, James Ogilvy, tennent ther, and Margaret Puller, his wife	0	12	0
Item, James Puller, shoemaker ther, and Isobell Skeen, his wife	0	18	0
Item, Arthur Toshech, tennent, in Elshilloch, his generall poll is	0	6	0
Item, Barbara William, his spouse	0	6	0
Item, George Ferrer, tennent ther, and Margaret Alexander, his wife	0	12	0
	£5	11	0

The valuation of the Laird of Glenkindies lands within the said parioch is an hundreth and fourty pounds Scots money	£140	0	0
The hundreth pairt whereof is	£1	8	0

(*Nota.*—This is not devided amongst the tennents in the Poll List given up, but is to be peyed be the heritor in a soume.)

(The Laird of Glenkendie doeth not receed within the parioch, therfor not pollable for himselfe nor familie heir.)

GLENCUIE.

Item, James Craige, tennent ther, and Isobell Forbes, his spouse, their poll is	£0	12	0

Item, Alaster, his son, his generall poll is	£0	6	0
Item, John Riach, tennent ther, and Bessie Morgan, his wife	0	12	0
Item, Alexander Rind, tennent ther, and Jannet Grassiach, his wife	0	12	0
Item, John Liet, tennent ther, and Jannet Elmslie, his wife	0	12	0
Item, Michael Dason, tennent there, and Elspet Gellan, his wife	0	12	0
Item, James Morgan, tennent ther, and Jannet Walker, his wife	0	12	0
Item, James Cowie, tennent in Pittandlich, his generall poll is	0	6	0
Item, James Reid, tennent ther, and Marjorie Roy, his spouse	0	12	0
Item, John Reid, his servant, his fee is £6 per annum, fortieth pairt whereof is 3s., and 6s. of generall poll	0	9	0
Item, Anna Morgan, his servant woman, her fee is £6 per annum, fortieth pairt whereof is 3s., and generall poll 6s., *inde* both is	0	9	0
Item, James Riach, tennent ther, and Jannet Mitchell, his spouse	0	12	0
Item, Donald Riach, tennent ther, and Agnes Hendry, his spouse	0	12	0
	£6	18	0

The LAIRD of SKELATERS valuatione within the parioch of Kinbetach is sixty pound Scots money.......... £60 0 0

The hundereth pairt whereof is.......... £0 12 0

(*Nota.*—This is not devided amongst the tennents in the poll list given up, but is to be peyed be the heretor in a soume.)

(Skellator does not receed in this parioch himselfe, therefor is not pollable for his familie.)

KINBETACH.

Imprimis, William Reid, tennent there, and Bessie Dason, his wife	£0	12	0
Item, John Dason, tennent ther, and Elspet Anderson, his spouse	0	12	0
Item, William Mulliert, tennent ther, and Jannet Marr, his wife	0	12	0
Item, William Luncart, tennent ther, and Jannet Nairne, his spouse	0	12	0
Item, Walter Dason, tennent ther, and Margrat Dason, his wife	0	12	0
Item, John Craigie, tennent ther, and Jean Moir, his spouse	0	12	0
Item, William Craigie, tennent ther, and Jannet Skeen, his spouse	0	12	0
Item, Bessie Rimer, his mother, generall poll is	0	6	0
Item, John Sumer, his servant, his fee is £6 per annum, fortieth pairt, with generall poll is	0	9	0
Item, Alaster Forbes, tennent ther, generall poll is	0	6	0
Item, Alexander Dason, tennent ther, and Agnes Grassach, his spouse	0	12	0
Item, John Michy, tennent ther, and Isobell Grassach, his spouse	0	12	0
	£6	9	0

The valluatione of ROBERT M'HARDIES lands in the said paroch is ane hundereth and sixty pounds Scots money.......... £160 0 0

The hundereth pairt whereof is.......... £1 12 0

(*Nota.*—This is not divyded amongst the tennents in the poll list given up, but is to be peyed in manner forsaid.)

(The said Robert M'Khardie doeth not receed within the said parioch, therefor not pollable for his familie.)

KINCLUNE.

	£	s.	d.
Imprimis, Alexander Watt, weaver ther, and Janet Reid, his spouse	£0	18	0
Item, Jannet Watt, his daughter, generall poll	0	6	0
Item, Alexander Reid, his servant, his fee is £8 per annum, fortieth part whereof is 4s., and generall poll 6s., *inde* both is	0	10	0
Item, James Cook, tennent ther, and Christian Lumsden, his spouse	0	12	0
Item, Alexander Garley, his servant, his fee is £10 per annum, fortieth part wherof is 5s., and generall poll 6s., *inde* both is	0	11	0
Item, Elspet Gibbon, his servant, her fee is £4 per annum, fortieth pairt whereof is 2s., and generall poll 6s., both is	0	8	0
Item, John Reid, tennent ther, and Barbara Leith, his spouse, their generall poll	0	12	0
Item, Alexander Glenny, tennent ther, and Elspet Forbes, his spouse	0	12	0
Item, James Glenny, tennent ther, and Margaret Bandon, his wife	0	12	0
Item, William Glenny, tennent ther, and Elspet Glenny, his wife	0	12	0
Item, John Beitty, tennent ther, and Margaret Ross, his wife, generall poll is	0	12	0
Item, Isobell Dason, a cottar woman	0	6	0
Item, John Gurly, cottar ther, generall poll	0	6	0
Beatrix Robertson, his wife, generall poll	0	6	0
	£7	3	0

CHARLES INNES of Belnaboth, his valuatione within the said parioch is fourty-fyve pound Scots £45 0 0

The hundereth part wherof extends to £0 9 6

(*Nota.*—This is not divyded amongst the tennents in the poll list given up, but is to be payed be the heretor in a soume.)

BELNABOTH.

	£	s.	d.
Imprimis, the said Charles Innes pays of poll	£3	6	0
Item, Margaret Forbes, his wife, and Isobell Innes, his daughter, their generall poll	0	12	0
Item, Alexander Raner, his servant, his fee is £13 6s. 8d. per annum, fortieth pairt whereof is 6s. 8d., and generall poll 6s., *inde* both is	0	12	8
Item, William Bredy, his servant, his fee is £13 6s. 8d. per annum, fortieth pairt whereof is 6s. 8d., and generall poll 6s., both is	0	12	8
Item, John Dason, his herd, his fee is £6 per annum, fortieth part, with generall poll	0	9	0
Item, James Murray, his servant, his fee is £6 per annum, fortieth pairt whereof is 3s., and generall poll 6s., both is	0	9	0

Item, Christian Anderson, his servant, fee £6 per annum, fortieth part, with generall poll	£0	9	0
Item Charles M'Donald, his herd, his fee is £4 per annum, fortieth pairt, and generall poll	0	8	0
Item, Patrick Divie, grassman ther, and Isobell Thomson, his spouse	0	12	0
	£17	10	4

JOHN INNES of Culquhich his valuatione within the said paroch is twenty pound, Scots money	£20	0	0
The hundreth pairt whereof is	£0	4	0

(*Nota.*—This is not divyded amongst the tennents in the poll list given up, but is to be payed in manner forsaid.)

(John Innes of Culquhich doeth not receed himself in this paroch, and therfor is not pollable for his familie heir.)

BURNES.

Imprimis, George Don, tennent ther, and Jannet Coutts, his wife, their generall poll is	£0	12	0
Item, Robert Mitchell, widower ther, his generall poll is	0	6	0
Item, Isobell Thomson, grasswoman, generall poll is	0	6	0
	£1	4	0

Summa of **KINBETHACK** paroch amounts to ane hundreth and twentie-six punds 14s. 4d.	£126	14	4

PARISH OF KINBETHOCK

OCCUPATIONS

Clerk & Collector	1	Laird	4
Commissioner	2	Millar	1
Cottar	4	Notar Publict	2
Gentleman	1	Servant Female	10
Grassman	1	Servant Male	29
Grasswoman	1	Shoemaker	2
Herd	1	Weaver	9
Lady	1		

PARISH OF KINBETHOCK

NAME (both sexes)	PAGE
ADAM Jannet	531
ALEXANDER Agnes	530
Jannet	529
Margaret	531
ANDERSON Alexander	529
Christian	534
Elspet	529(2),532
James	529
Margaret	529
Robert	530
William	529
BANDAN Margaret	527
Patrick	527
BANDON Elspet	527
John	527
Margaret	533
BAXTER Isobell	531
BEITTIE Robert	527
BEITTY John	533
Margaret	533
Thomas	528
BERRY Adam	529
Margaret	529
BONNAR Marjorie	528
BREDY Alexander	529
Christian	531
George	531
Jannet	529
Margaret	527
William	533
BRODY Duncan	527
Elspet	527
John	527
BRUX Laird of	528(2)
BULKY Jannet	527
CANDACH Christian	527
CLERK George	528
Isobel	528
William	528(2)
CONNEN Jannet	529
COOK Christian	533
Isobell	528
James	533
Margaret	531
COUPLAND John	529
Margaret	529
COUTS Isobell	530
Margaret	528
Mary	528
COUTTS Alaster	529

NAME (both sexes)	PAG
COUTTS Alexander	53
Christian	53
Elspet	52
Isobell	529,53
Jannet	529,53
John	52
Margaret	53
Robert	52
COWIE James	53
Janet	53
CRAIGE Alaster	53
Isobell	53
James	53
CRAIGIE Alexander	52
Isobell	52
Jannet	529,53
Jean	529,53
John	529,53
William	53
CRAIGIVAR Laird of	530(
CRIMON Margaret	52
DASON Agnes	53
Alexander	528,53
Bessie	53
Elspet	527,528,532(
Isobell	53
James	52
Jannet	5
John	532,53
Margrat	53
Michael	5
Walter	53
DINKISON Agnes	53
Alexander	53
Jeane	53
John	53
DIVIE Isobell	53
Patrick	53
DON George	53
Isobell	52
Jannet	5
John	52
DUN William	5
DUNBAR Anna	52
DUNCAN Alaster	5
Beatrix	5
Christian	5
Elspet	52
George	527,5
James	5
Robert	5

PARISH OF KINBETHOCK

IAME (both sexes)	PAGE
UNCAN William	529
UWIE Jannet	531
LMSLIE Alexander	529
Isobell	529
Jannet	532
ERRER Francis	531
George	531
Isobell	529
John	529
Margaret	531
ORBES Alaster	532
Alexander	530
Anna	531
Arthour	529
Arthur	530
Elspet	529,530,533
Isobell	530,531
Jean	530,531
John	526,531
Margaret	527,529,531,533
Marjorie	529
Mary	528
Patrick	528
William	527(2),529(2)
RBESS Isobell	529
FE Charles	527
William	528
RLEY Alexander	533
LLAN Elspet	532
BBON Elspet	533
Jannet	527
Margaret	527(2)
Robert	527
William	527
ASS Margaret	529
ASSIAN Alaster	529
Arthour	529
Jannet	529
Marjorie	529
ENKINDIE Laird of	531(2)
ENNY Alexander	533
Barbara	527
Elspet	533(2)
James	533
Margaret	528,533
Thomas	528
William	533
RDON Marjorie	528
RDONE John	528

NAME (both sexes)	PAGE
GORDONE Margaret	528
GOW John	528
GRANT Jean	529
Thomas	529
GRASSACH Agnes	532
Isobell	532
GRASSIACH Beatrix	529,530
Jannet	530,532
GRAY Lucriss	528
GURLY Beatrix	533
John	533
HENDERSON Barbara	527
John	527
HENDRY Agnes	532
Margaret	529
INNES Alexander	528
Charles	526,533(2)
Isobell	533
John	526,534(2)
Lucriss	528
Margaret	533
JAFFRAY George	530
Janet	530
KELLS Margaret	528
KERR Elspet	530
KNIGHT Isobell	531
LAING Jean	530
LAMON Margaret	527
LAW Margaret	528,529
William	529
LEITCH Elspet	528
LEITH Barbara	533
Isobell	528
Patrick	528
LIET Jannet	532
John	532
LUMSDEN Christian	533
LUNCART Elspet	530
James	530
Jannet	532
William	532
MAIR William	527
MARR Jannet	532
Lady Duager of	526(3)
MCDONALD Charles	534
MCFARLAND Walter	529

PARISH OF KINBETHOCK

NAME (both sexes)	PAGE
MCGRIGOR Alaster	529
Elspet	529
MCHARDIE Robert	532,533
MCROBIE Christian	527
MESSER Alexander	530
Jean	530
MICHELL Isobell	531
MICHY Isobell	532
Jean	530
John	532
MILNE Anna	531
Lachlan	531
MITCHELL Christian	527
Jannet	532
John	527
Robert	534
MOIR Jean	532
MORGAN Anna	532
Bessie	532
Elspet	529
Isobell	528,531
James	532
Jannet	532
John	531
MORTIMER Alexander	527
James	527
Margaret	527
MULLIERT Jannet	532
William	532
MUNZIE Elspet	527
George	530
MURISON Adam	530
Ewan	530
Jannet	530
Margaret	530
Marjorie	530
MURRAY James	533
NAIRN William	531
NAIRNE Jannet	532
OGILVY James	531
Margaret	531
PANTON Elspet	530
PULLER Isobell	531
James	531
Margaret	531
RAEBURN Isobell	528
RAINE Alaster	530
RANER Alexander	533

NAME (both sexes)	PAG
REID Agnes	5
Alexander	5
Anna	5
Barbara	5
Bessie	5
Christian	5
Elspet	5
Issobell	5
James	529,5
Janet	5
Jannet	5
Jean	5
John	528,532,5
Margaret	528,5
Marjorie	528,5
Patrick	5
Robert	5
William	527,529,5
RIACH Agnes	5
Bessie	5
Donald	5
James	5
Jannet	5
Jean	5
John	5
RIMER Bessie	5
RIND Alexander	5
Jannet	5
RITCHY Elspet	5
Margaret	5
ROBERTSON Beatrix	5
Isobell	5
ROSS Margaret	529,5
ROY Marjorie	5
SHAW Jean	5
John	5
SHIRRAFF James	5
Margaret	5
SKEEN Isobell	5
Jannet	5
SKELATER Laird of	5
SKELLATOR Laird of	5
SMITH Agnes	5
Elspet	5
Margaret	5
Patrick	5
STEPHAN Christian	5
STRACHAN Charles	5
Margaret	5
Patrick	5
STRACHEN Anna	5

PARISH OF KINBETHOCK

NAME (both sexes)	PAGE
STRACHEN Thomas	528
SUMER Isobell	529
James	529
John	532
TAILZIOR Margaret	530
THOMSON Alexander	529,531
Arthour	529
Arthur	531
Beatrix	529
Isobell	530,531,534(2)
James	528
Jannet	531
Marjorie	528
TOMB Alexander	527
TOSHECH Arthur	530,531
Barbara	531
Jannet	531
TOUCH William	527
WALKER Alexander	527,529
Andrew	527
Anna	529
Elspet	529

NAME (both sexes)	PAGE
WALKER Jannet	529,532
John	529
Margaret	527
Marjorie	528
WATT Alexander	533
Janet	533
Jannet	528,533
John	528
Marjorie	528
William	528
WILLIAM Agnes	531
Alexander	531
Barbara	531
George	531(2)
James	531
John	531(2)
Margaret	531
WILSONE George	527
WRIGHT Elspet	529
William	530
YOOL Isobell	528
William	528

PARISH OF KINBETHOCK

PLACE NAME		PAGE
BELNABOTH		526,533(2)
BLAIRS		528
BRUX		528(2)
BURNES		534
CALQUHICH		526
CLOSHCUNIE		529
COOKHILL		528
CORRIHILL		528
CRAIGIVAR		530(2)
CULFORK		529
	Milne of	529
CULQUHICH		534(2)
CUSHLAIHIE		529
DEN		528
DRUMALACHIE	Nether	527
	Upper	527
ELSHILLOCH		531
FOULES		529
FUCHLIE		527
GLENCUIE		531
GLENKINDIE		531(2)
HAUGHTOUNE		530
KINBETACH		526(2),530,532(2)
KINBETHACK		534
KINCLUNE		533
KNOWHEAD		527
LEY		527
MARR		526(3)
MORLICHIE	New	528
	Old	528
NEWBIGGING		528
PITTANDLICH		532
SINABOTH		530
SKELATER		532
SKELLATOR		532
STYCROFTS		529
SUNAHARD	Upper	531
SUNAHARDS		531
TORRIECARN		529
TOUNE	Old	529
TOWIE		526
	Maines of	530
	Milne of	528
	Uper	529
TOWY	Nether	529